MODERN RIVALS
TO
CHRISTIAN
FAITH

THE LAYMAN'S THEOLOGICAL LIBRARY
ROBERT McAFEE BROWN, *General Editor*

Modern Rivals
to
Christian
Faith

by
Cornelius Loew

LAYMAN'S
THEOLOGICAL
LIBRARY

THE WESTMINSTER PRESS

PHILADELPHIA

Acknowledgment is made for permission to quote from the following:

PEACE OF MIND, by Joshua Loth Liebman. Simon & Schuster, Inc., 1946.

PEACE WITH GOD, by Billy Graham. Copyright 1953 by Billy Graham, reprinted by permission of Doubleday & Company, Inc.

THE POWER OF POSITIVE THINKING, by Norman Vincent Peale. Copyright 1952 by Prentice-Hall, Inc.

KIERKEGAARD, by Walter Lowrie. Oxford University Press, 1938.

Scripture quotations from the Revised Standard Version of the Bible are copyright, 1946 and 1952, and are used by permission.

Library of Congress Catalog Card Number: 56–6173

PRINTED IN THE UNITED STATES OF AMERICA

Contents

Foreword   7

PART ONE: ALTERNATIVES TO CHRISTIANITY
              IN AMERICAN LIFE

1. " Where Your Treasure Is . . ."   9
2. " Science Is the Measure . . ."   15
3. " Democracy Is the Measure . . ."   29
4. " The Nation Is the Measure . . ."   43

PART TWO: IDOLATRY " INSIDE CHRISTIANITY "

5. The " Return to Religion "   52
6. The Protestant Reformers and " Christian Idolatry "   63
7. " Making the Most of Yourself " Christianity   71
8. The Tradition Within the Traditions   81
9. Where Do We Go from Here?   92

References   96

FOREWORD

The religious book market is full of books for "the intelligent layman." Some are an insult to his intelligence. Others are covertly written for professional theologians. A few are genuine helps in communicating the faith.

In this spate of books being thrust at the lay reader, what distinctive place can the Layman's Theological Library claim to hold? For one thing, it will try to remind the layman that he *is* a theologian. The close conjunction of the words "layman" and "theological" in the title of the series is not by chance but by design. For theology is not an irrelevant pastime of seminary professors. It is the occupation of every Christian, the moment he begins to think about, or talk about, or communicate, his Christian faith. The injunction to love God *with all his mind,* necessarily involves the layman in theology. He can never avoid theology; if he refuses to think through his faith, he simply settles for inferior theology.

Furthermore, the Layman's Theological Library will attempt to give a *wholeness* in its presentation of the Christian faith. Its twelve volumes cover the main areas of Christian faith and practice. They are written out of similar convictions which the authors share about the uniqueness of the Christian faith. All the authors are convinced that Christian faith can

7

be made relevant, that it can be made understandable without becoming innocuous, and that (particularly in view of the current "return to religion") it is crucially important for the layman to commit himself to more than "religion in general." The Layman's Theological Library, then, will attempt a fresh exploration of the Christian faith, and what it can mean in the life of twentieth-century man.

The present volume not only stands upon its own feet, but also introduces the series as a whole. Dr. Loew examines various rivals to Christian faith on the contemporary scene, and in the course of his discussion indicates many of the ingredients of an authentic faith which must replace these rivals. The rivals exist not only outside of Christian faith, but, even more dangerously, within Christian faith itself.

The battle with the "false gods" is never done, and part of our ability to recognize the true God will depend upon the degree to which we can dethrone the pretenders to his claims. In this all-important battle, Dr. Loew's book can be an effective weapon.

Robert McAfee Brown

PART ONE: *Alternatives to Christianity in American Life*

CHAPTER

1

"WHERE YOUR TREASURE IS . . ."

At least ninety-five per cent of all adult Americans believe in God and seventy-five per cent regard themselves as members of churches. More than fifty per cent of those who count themselves church members say they attend services with some regularity. These findings of recent public opinion polls seem to tell us that there is no basis even to suspect that there are in America today live, powerful religious alternatives to Christianity.

The picture of the religious situation in the United States will change before our very eyes, however, if we sharpen our definition of religion and relate it more closely to what actually goes on in our day-to-day living.

What is religion? Religion can be thought of primarily in terms of beliefs. A "real Christian" often is described as a person who believes certain doctrines — that God is the Creator, that Jesus Christ is the Son of God, that the Bible is the authoritative Word of God, that Jesus was born of a virgin, and so on. Such a person is "orthodox," which simply means that he or she holds the "right beliefs."

But many of us react against this approach. We have great difficulty making sense out of all the so-called "right beliefs" taught by the Christian churches down through the centuries. We wonder whether it makes much difference what a person believes as long as he or she " lives right." We would rather describe a Christian as a person who follows a certain way of life — for instance, one who lives by the Golden Rule. Yet a moment's reflection will reveal that we are fooling ourselves if we think that this " practical" approach avoids beliefs. Whether he realizes it or not, any person who is serious about living by the Golden Rule is guided and motivated by certain beliefs about himself, about other people, and about the very meaning and purpose of life itself. At the very least, he believes that the good life means getting along well with other people and that it pays to be good. He also believes that he and the persons with whom he lives are capable of doing unto others as they would have others do unto them. This is a very important belief, and it cannot be taken for granted. Behind every pattern of practical living there are basic attitudes and convictions. These attitudes and convictions add up to a set of " right beliefs" even though they may not be expressed in word formulas like the Christian doctrines mentioned above.

The idea that a belief is religious all by itself, however, can be misleading. No belief is truly religious for any of us unless it exerts an actual influence on our living. So let us ask, What makes a belief religious? The answer is that a belief *becomes* religious when it performs a special job in a person's life. Here are three statements, each of which describes this special job in a slightly different way:

1. Any belief becomes religious when it acts like the core of a magnet, drawing together the lines of force of an individual's personality into an effective pattern.

Example: statement by John H. Dietrich, pioneer religious humanist: " For centuries the idea of God has been the very heart of religion; it has been said, ' No God, no religion.' But humanism thinks of religion as something very different and far deeper than any belief in God. To it, religion is not the attempt to establish right relations with a supernatural being, but rather the upreaching and aspiring impulse in a human life. It is life striving for its completest fulfillment, and anything which contributes to this fulfillment is religious, whether it be associated with the idea of God or not."

2. Any belief becomes religious when a person gives his supreme loyalty to the interest this belief represents and subordinates all of his other interests to this one interest.

Example: words written by a British pilot, killed in action, in a letter his mother was to read in case he did not return: " My death would not mean that your struggle had been in vain. Far from it. It means that your sacrifice is as great as mine. Those who serve England must expect nothing from her; we debase ourselves if we regard our country as merely a place in which to eat and sleep. . . .

" However long time may be, one thing can never be altered — I shall have lived and died an Englishman. Nothing else matters one jot, nor can anything ever change it."

3. Any belief becomes religious when it provides a meaning for living to which a person clings in the face of all challenge, competition, denial, and suffering.

Example: words written by the apostle Paul in a letter to Christians at Rome. " I am sure that neither death, nor life, nor angels, nor principalities, nor things present, nor things to come, nor powers, nor height, nor depth, nor anything else in all creation, will be able to separate us from the love of God in Christ Jesus our Lord." (Rom. 8:37-39.)

The distinctive mark of religion is not *what* a person believes, but *how* he believes. *No* belief is religious unless it is energized by the attitude of commitment, loyalty, devotion. *Any* belief supported by this attitude is religious, " whether it is associated with the idea of God or not." In other words, beliefs that we usually consider irreligious may be held religiously, and Christian beliefs may be held irreligiously.

Let us push this line of thought to the most shocking conclusion we can think of: A devoted Communist is more vitally "religious" than a lukewarm Christian. How can this be? Does not Communism officially deny the reality of God and attack religion as the opiate of the people? Yet look at the contrast here. Lukewarm Christians give lip service to Christian beliefs concerning God without giving God their deepest loyalty. Dedicated Communists give their heart and soul and mind and strength to an atheistic movement. Obviously these Communists are very "religious," even though their religion is a false religion.

What about lukewarm Christians? Undoubtedly they are religious too. But the point is that their *real* religion, the commitments that actually shape the pattern of their living, are located somewhere else than in the Christian beliefs which they hold so lightly. If we can discover what it is that excites their devotion and captures their active concern, we shall be entering their "holy of holies" and meeting their real "gods."

Some people are lukewarm Christians because for one reason or another they do not discipline themselves toward any overarching loyalty that engages their entire heart and soul and mind and strength. They live for family, business, nation, social position, comfort, assorted other things, and God — all at the same time, with varying degrees of interest and concern in various situations. When Father is pulling off a big business deal, the outcome is a life-and-death matter and nothing is quite so important as success. When vacation time rolls around, or when there is sickness in the family, all interest centers on family affairs. When the cold war threatens to become hot, a tremor of fear and anxiety runs through the heart and everything seems to depend on national and international affairs. When all these things are happening simultaneously, there is confusion, and " going to church " does not necessarily bring order out of chaos. Persons who fail to establish a priority system of commitments discover sooner or later that their energies are not focused and that their pattern of living is blurred. To put it in religious language, they worship *many gods* instead of bringing themselves and all of their concerns under the guidance and power of *one god*.

But worship of *one god* does not guarantee worship of the one *true* God who claims the supreme loyalty of Christians. Some people are passionately devoted to a *single* basic concern which dominates their practical living. There are fathers who consistently make their business or profession the object of primary loyalty and who systematically subordinate everything else to achievement, advancement, and success in their field. There are mothers who always without exception judge every event and every activity in terms of the interests and welfare of their family. Some individuals exalt the sheer enjoyment of life and make the pursuit of pleasure into the " something " which all other facets of living must serve. Or at the other extreme, some individuals make living carefully according to a definite set of " do's " and " don'ts " the be-all and end-all of their life. In fact, any special interest can act as a magnetic core, drawing all other interests into a pattern: a white person becomes wholly immersed in the effort to stave off the movement of the Negro people toward full equality; a believer in democracy becomes totally engrossed in defending democracy against the threat of Communism; a 100-per-cent American becomes a fanatical crusader for the preservation of his country's right to do what it likes as long as it has the power to brush aside opposition. The list could go on and on.

Jesus once said, " Where your treasure is, there will your

heart be also " (Matt. 6:21). Here, concentrated into a single sentence, is the view of religion we have been talking about. We give our loyalty, commitment, devotion, to whatever means most to us and concerns us most deeply. The practical question, then, is whether we worship the one *true* God with all our heart and soul and mind and strength, or whether we put in God's place some interest or concern or movement or program that is less than God. The Bible calls any such substitute an *idol* and any such religion *idolatry*.

By this time it should be obvious that we cannot understand the religious situation in our country by looking at statistics on church membership, church attendance, and " belief in God." We must ask, " What God or gods do Americans *actually* worship? "

The purpose of tracking down idols and bringing them out into the open is positive, not negative. Criticism is necessary to the life of faith, for unless we are aware of what false faith is we cannot do the truth which true faith requires. But it is equally true that we cannot identify idols unless we have a " yardstick." Therefore the real purpose of this book is to challenge the reader to rediscover the full message of the Bible and Christian tradition *in its totality*. To put it in terms of our previous discussion of religion, although it is not *what* a person believes but *how* he believes it that makes a belief religious, Christian faith combines the *what* and the *how*: it not only commands the " how " — " You shall worship the Lord your God and him only shall you serve " — but it also proclaims the " what " — " God was in Christ reconciling the world to himself." The Christian struggle *against* idolatry makes sense only when it is a struggle *for* complete loyalty to the one true God, as he has revealed himself.

"SCIENCE IS THE MEASURE . . ."

The word "scientific" has great authority among us. Think for a moment of the automatic way we react favorably to this word:

If something is done "scientifically," it is done well.

If a product is made "scientifically," it is good.

If a question is studied "scientifically," the answer is correct.

If a problem is attacked "scientifically," a practical solution will be discovered sooner or later.

Not one of these statements is *necessarily* true, yet it is difficult for us not to agree with them.

Our reverence for science is entirely reasonable, for the history of modern science is a story of doing the impossible. Every generation of scientists since Galileo and Newton has achieved a level of knowledge and power which previously had been thought to be beyond human ability. If these great men were to visit us today, they would be astounded by the tremendous advances that have been made since their time. Looking at our world of electricity, atomic power, helicopters, TV sets, polio vaccine, skyscrapers, automobiles, and all the other marvels that are included in "the American standard of living," they might well say, "If this is what can be done in three short centuries, after human civilization had been plugging along for more than sixty centuries, absolutely nothing should be impossible in the future!"

Many Americans believe that the story of modern science is the most significant story in the whole of human history. In the light of rapid improvements in so many areas, they tend to look down on the earlier ages of mankind as ignorant, superstitious, and unprogressive. This is one reason why some people suspect that science is the funeral director who has buried traditional Christianity in the cemetery of human errors. The fact that Christianity is an "ancient" rather than a "modern" movement puts two strikes against it. Another reason why people who have deep respect for science often wonder about the place of Christianity in our modern world is that they have heard so much about "the so-called 'warfare between science and religion.'"

But there is a more important reason why many Americans consider "the Christianity of creeds and doctrines" out of date. *The success of science offers a new religion in place of Christianity*. The creed of this religion can be summarized in a single sentence: Not only can science create a society free from hunger, poverty, disease, and ignorance, but beyond that, science can provide an understanding of life which will satisfy men's deepest needs and resolve their basic conflicts. What is this understanding of life? It is the confidence that sooner or later we human beings will solve *every* major problem of mind and spirit, provided we apply to these problems the same scientific ingenuity that has unlocked the innermost secrets of the physical universe.

This is the faith that science inspires. Confidence in human self-sufficiency lies back of the feeling that Christianity does not really fit into the modern world. What have heaven, hell, salvation, atonement, eternal life, judgment, sin, and forgiveness to do with a technological society controlled by men and women who believe that they are on the way to solving all their problems? These ancient words refer to deep-seated difficulties which are taken seriously only by persons who are willing to admit that they are not self-sufficient. They answer questions that persons who think they can solve all their basic problems do not ask.

Wonderful as it is, the environment we have created through the power of science tempts us to disregard pride, selfishness, anger, envy, hate, greed, lust for power, death, and the like, which Christian tradition tells us we cannot handle by means of our own abilities and efforts and techniques. Our environment encourages us to respond to the promise and hope of a way of life in which we rely wholly on ourselves and on our fellow men. In fact, it makes many of us feel that any person who seriously "turns to God" and becomes ardent in his traditional faith must be weak or inadequate in some way. The ideal of being self-reliant is so strong in our culture that we seldom escape the suspicion that religion is a crutch — all religion, that is, except a faith based on confidence in ourselves as mature individuals who can co-operate with one another to build the good life.

Usually a person who is consciously devoted to a view of life based on reverence for science (let's call him a "humanist" for the sake of convenience) will not agree that he believes in a religion. Probably he thinks that he does not worship anything. He does not pray to any power greater than himself from whom he believes he receives guidance and support. He does not belong to any organized community of believers. So his actual religion, his "working faith," is hidden beneath the notion that he has no religion. What does his faith look like when it is brought to the surface? What makes it "tick"?

Suppose we listen in on a conversation between a humanist and a Christian. The two have struck up a casual acquaintance while traveling by train from Chicago to New York, and each man is favorably impressed by the other. They are ready to talk about things that mean a lot to them.

CHRISTIAN: A few minutes ago you used the phrase "narrow-minded religionists." I would be interested to know whether you think that all " religionists " are narrow-minded. I'm an active member of a church — Presbyterian, to be exact — and although I cannot say that I always am satisfied with what I hear in church, I don't believe that what I hear is narrow-minded.

HUMANIST: Well, what bothers me about Christianity is that you have to accept certain matters laid down long ago as though they were true for all time. Now I take my cue from science. It seems to me that science has taught us what it means to be open-minded. It says that all of our knowledge is temporary and therefore our ideas and beliefs will have to change as we learn more. This kind of open-mindedness means that I must be willing to give up my most cherished beliefs when new discoveries disprove them. You cannot take that attitude.

CHRISTIAN: I don't see why I cannot take that attitude. The way I look at it, there is a big difference between saying that my faith makes me narrow-minded and saying that I am narrow-minded about my faith. Certainly the business of making connections between the traditional doctrines of my church and my everyday life is not easy. But I do not accept these doctrines as a package of information forced on me. They are clues to what life is all about, and the question of being narrow-minded or open-minded is a question of how I apply them to my actual living. I may value some particular interpretation of these clues so much that I become dogmatic and intolerant. If this happens, then it is a good thing when my interpretation is challenged. So far as science is concerned, I am every bit as interested in progress and change as you are. My drug business depends on scientific methods and new discoveries.

HUMANIST: You do not understand my criticism. You are open-minded about results in particular fields like chemistry, but you are not facing the real challenge with which *science* confronts religion.

CHRISTIAN: All right. Lay it on the line.

HUMANIST: Let me tell you about my own experience. I used to go to church regularly until I was in my teens. I heard over and over again that there is a God who watches over every one of us personally, who sees everything we do even when nobody is around, who has a plan for every life, and who created the whole universe just so that men could be born on this planet to worship and obey him. The older I grew the more I wondered how my parents and Sunday school teachers and the minister *knew* all these things. I never got an answer that went much beyond the song I had memorized when I was in kindergarten: " Jesus loves me, this I know, for the Bible tells me so." My impression was that everything a person needs to know about life was decided long ago and written down once for all.

CHRISTIAN: So far, we are brothers. My early religious training was very similar to yours.

HUMANIST: Now wait a minute. I'm telling the story.

CHRISTIAN: Excuse me. Go right ahead.

HUMANIST: Thank you. In high school and college I came in contact with a picture of the universe that was much more convincing than the Bible. It was built on *real* knowledge, on facts that had been tested scientifically. I learned that we have no evidence that the universe has an over-all purpose or that anyone beyond the universe has any concern for us. We have no evidence that human beings are special favorites for whom the universe has been evolving for three billion years. On the contrary, science has demonstrated more and more convincingly that we men have been produced by the same natural processes that have produced all other things, and that we are subject to the same regular laws that govern stars and rocks and plants and animals.

Ever since that time I have operated on the principle that *nothing can be believed unless it can be proved*. I gave up my early belief in God for the same reason I stopped believing in elves and fairies. For the life of me, I cannot understand how you can hang on to traditional religion if you really are open to the implications of science!

CHRISTIAN: Well, I guess I still believe in God because I do not agree that the question of fairies and elves is the same as the question of God's reality. God is absolutely central to the meaning of my life; fairies and elves are not. I cannot put God on display publicly or prove his reality by lab experiments. Yet I believe that I have experienced the presence and support and guidance and criticism of God. Sometimes I run into facts or problems that confuse me and make me doubt, but I cannot go all the way and deny the reality of God. The apostle Paul put it very well when he said that we walk by faith and not by sight. I don't think it is fair for you to dismiss my deepest experiences simply because I cannot prove something which I admit from the beginning cannot be proved.

HUMANIST: What you say is very interesting. You have reminded me of another reason why I hold to the rule that what can't be proved can't be believed. To put it bluntly, I wonder why belief in God is so important to you. It seems to me that you are *too interested* in the reality of God. The sciences of psychology and sociology have come up with some pretty uncomplimentary explanations of why people get wrapped up in religion.

CHRISTIAN: I feel that you are putting me on the defensive, but I think I can take it. What bitter pill have psychology and sociology been manufacturing?

HUMANIST: Please don't take what I am going to say personally. I certainly don't know you well enough to start passing judgment on your reasons for doing anything, let alone your reasons for being a Christian. But since we have gone this far, let me tell you what the scientific studies show. People cling to beliefs about the support and guidance of God because they *want* to believe, and not because they *know* that the beliefs are true. They experience " divine support and guidance," all right, but where do these experiences come from? We do not have any proof that there is a " Heavenly Father " who takes care of us, but we do have a large number of case histories of persons who create " religious experiences " by means of their own imaginations. Why do they do this? Because they cannot stand on their own two feet and meet their problems. They use religious ideas and images to cover up their ignorance about what is really going on in their lives, to quiet their fears and to bolster their hopes.

CHRISTIAN: This may be true in a few cases. In fact, I am sure that it is. What has this to do with normal church life?

HUMANIST: You are forcing me to be hard-boiled. I'm going to press my point home. Why is it that so many church members seem to believe that religion is a consolation for those who are mourning or who are having a rough time in some other way, but that it is not very important for them as long as they enjoy smooth sailing? Why do some of us suspect — and I think figures would back us up — that the churches are supported more enthusiastically by unadjusted persons than by successful ones, by unmarried women more than by those happily married, by men who have difficulty triumphing in the dog-eat-dog business world, by persons who are lonely rather than by those who have plenty of friends? How can you be sure that your religion is anything more than a badge of immaturity which you wear because you don't have confidence in yourself? How can you be sure that you aren't fooling yourself?

CHRISTIAN: I'm going to toss the ball right back to you. How do *you* keep from fooling *yourself*?

HUMANIST: That's a fair question. I try to keep from fooling myself by not expecting any outside help. If I did experience the feeling of being supported or guided by a power beyond myself, I would give the credit to *society,* because I *know* that society influences me constantly without my being aware of it. But I still would be suspicious of all such feelings. The only way I can become the completely grown-up person I ought to be is to have confidence in myself and not look for any outside agent to step in and solve my problems for me.

CHRISTIAN: If I were convinced, as you seem to be, that Christianity offers to free people from the burden of making their own decisions and gives them illusions of security, I would not want anything to do with it either. Perhaps you think that I believe all religion is " a good thing " and that all we need is more religion. On the contrary, I believe that healthy religion is the best thing in life, but that unhealthy religion is just about the worst. You have described a self-centered, unhealthy type of faith. Healthy faith involves the courage to affirm God even when we don't get a thing out of it for ourselves — except perhaps some tensions and insecurities that otherwise we would try to avoid.

HUMANIST: Well said. It's striking that you feel religion gives you the attitude I get from science. We both want to be honest and let the chips fall where they may. But don't you see? — science deals with facts that are the same for everybody, while even the " healthy religion " you defend is such a private affair that there is no sure way of separating fact from fancy. That is the main reason why religion does not offer a solid base for solving human problems. On the other hand, scientists can separate fact from fancy, and therefore they are able to describe problems as they really exist and to discover ways of doing something about them. For instance, it does no one any good to think that cancer is incurable, and it certainly does not help to preach that cancer ought to be cured. We have to make enough money available so that careful, patient study of the disease can be carried on long enough so that a cure will be found.

This is the way we ought to approach all our problems. Every time I think of how much energy has gone into preaching about moral or religious ideals instead of testing them in actual practice I feel depressed. The vast majority of people want to be good and do the right thing. Every person knows down deep in his heart that he ought to love his neighbor as himself. That is not the main problem. The problem is that people give mere lip service to their ideals because they do not know how to put their ideals into action. As we *learn* more about ourselves and about society through science we will *do* more. There is no problem area of human living that we cannot improve if we study the causes of the difficulty carefully enough and invent the proper techniques for making whatever changes are necessary. It is just a matter of time and effort and education.

The Christian has much to say, but we have heard enough of the conversation to realize that the humanist is a sincere, concerned, and deeply religious person. He is not lukewarm. He has outlined a philosophy of life which is congenial to millions of Americans not only outside but also inside the churches. Probably he has thought through his position more consistently than many of us are in the habit of doing, but this simply means that he may have helped us to see more clearly than usual certain ideas and attitudes that we hold ourselves. However, one thing the humanist does not see is his own faith, and now we are going to bring it to the surface.

First of all, we should note that the humanist is not so completely open-minded as he thinks he is. He bases his outlook on several beliefs which he doggedly refuses to give up. He treats the following beliefs as though they really cannot be doubted by any reasonable person:

1. Nothing can be believed unless it can be proved scientifically.

2. Human beings must rely wholly upon themselves and on one another in achieving maturity and fullness of life.

3. Science has accomplished so much already that we can expect it to help us solve all problems eventually.

But has any one of these beliefs been proved scientifically? No, and for a very good reason. Every one of them goes *beyond information about facts* and *interprets the facts* in a certain way in order to support an over-all approach to life. This is an illustration of one of the basic " facts of life," which is that all convictions about the meaning of life are interpretations of human experience which cannot be " proved." They are clues we use to make sense out of the countless facts we encounter and which we can study scientifically. Or to use a word picture, they are like a pair of glasses. We all wear glasses and we see everything through them. We cannot prove that we are wearing the right glasses. We cannot prove that the glasses we have decided to wear focus our eyes clearly and truly. We have to take a risk. Now the humanist does not want to take this risk, and he thinks that science eliminates the risk. He casts science in the role of an eye doctor who can test our glasses and tell us whether we see straight.

Science is among the noblest achievements of man, but it cannot play the role of the eye doctor. Its proper role is to search for the kind of knowledge that will give us control over the forces and processes of the physical universe, and it has played this role sensationally. In his enthusiasm for science, the humanist has forgotten that *science is a tool*. Tools are invented by men, they are made by men, and they are used by men. Tools can be used constructively, but also destructively. Science places power in our hands, but it does not decide how that power is going to be used. Why was it that many of the scientists who worked on the problem of releasing and controlling atomic energy were deeply disturbed about the awesome power they were unleashing and warned us that fateful decisions would have to be made about the future use of atomic energy? Certainly one reason was that there is nothing in science *as science* which can settle the profound moral issues involved in revolutionary discoveries.

The humanist has drawn certain implications from the methods of science and from the scientific picture of the universe which he finds very convincing, and apparently he does not realize that he is interpreting scientific information rather than simply accepting knowledge " proved " by science. All this adds up to the conclusion that the humanist fails to stick by his own principle that what can't be proved can't be believed. His basic assumptions cannot be proved, and therefore he is taking the risk of faith that all the rest of us have to take, even though he thinks that he has side-stepped the necessity of walking by faith rather than by sight.

We are ready for the main question. What actually is the humanist's supreme loyalty? What is his god? Let us look again at his three basic beliefs:

1. Nothing can be believed unless it can be proved scientifically.

2. Human beings must rely wholly upon themselves and on one another in achieving maturity and fullness of life.

3. Science has accomplished so much already that we can expect it to help us solve all problems eventually.

The center of gravity clearly rests on the middle belief; the other two support it. Belief number one leaves man standing alone in the center of the stage by automatically canceling out God because God cannot be proved to exist. Belief number three gives added support to the notion that man is the sole manager of his own destiny by emphasizing the fact that the astounding achievements of modern science are achievements of human beings. It says that the hope of man is man.

The god of the humanist is man. Man, using the instrument of science which he has invented, is the measure of all things. Although the humanist may resent being told that he worships man, his devotion to science as the power unto salvation speaks louder than many pious words or much bending of the knee.

But we must go a step farther. How does the humanist define man? What is the character of this object of worship? The humanist pictures man as basically good, seriously concerned about truth, democracy, and social justice, and motivated by the ideal of loving his neighbor as himself. Where does he get this picture? It is not based on a scientific survey of the human race. A survey would show that for every man who is seriously concerned about truth, democracy, and social justice, there are plenty more who use truth or falsehood interchangeably and who are more concerned about " What's in it for me? " than about loving their neighbor. This is a portrait of the humanist himself, a self-portrait. His hope for the future really rests on the hope that through time, effort, and education there will be more people like him. Thus the humanist not only worships man, but he makes man in his own image. (*Important note to Christians:* Idolizing oneself is not something that is peculiar to humanists. When self-righteous Christians piously announce that " if only every one were Christian — like them, of course! — the world would be a much better place to live in," they are doing the very same thing.)

You will remember that in his conversation with the Christian, the humanist tried to " explain away " the Christian's belief in God by suggesting that religious experiences are produced by people themselves to compensate for ignorance, to quiet fears, and to bolster hope. Could it be that the humanist must speak with glowing optimism in the name of science because he cannot bear to face *all* the " facts of life "?

Faith in man based on reverence for science is a live alternative to Christianity. But it is more than that. It is a temptation to professing Christians. Every one of us has been influenced immensely by the strong scientific emphasis in modern life and by the spectacular success of the sciences. The conversation between the humanist and the Christian goes on right inside of us. Who wins? Unless we are willing to engage in the discipline of vigorous debate and careful thinking, such as has been outlined in this chapter, the chances are that we will not know.

The identification of idols is no easy or comfortable job because the question whether something or someone less than God is being given God's rightful place in life has a way of circling back to our own doorstep. This is as it should be. Tracking down one's own idols is a necessary part of trying to be a Christian. The goal, remember, is positive, not negative. We must not seek to unmask idolatry in order to " show up " other people or to torture ourselves in the vain hope that this is what Christ meant when he said that we must " take up our cross." The search for idols is a form of spiritual surgery. It hurts only so that it may heal. The goal is a vital, consistent, courageous, triumphant Christian faith which is not weakened by divided loyalities.

During the Second World War a Navy chaplain preached a power-packed sermon on the Ten Commandments. One sailor in the congregation was transfixed and devastated by the catalogue of " thou shalt nots." He left the service very much depressed by a consciousness of having done evil in the sight of the Lord all up and down the line. But soon he brightened and said to himself, " Well, at least I've never made a graven image." Probably he was wrong. For what is a graven (hand-made) image in modern terms? Anything that man has created. If we worship ourselves or anything that we have created, we are bowing down to an idol. Those of us who idolize the success of modern science — and once again, who of us does not do this to some extent? — are breaking the Second Commandment: " You shall not make yourself a graven image, or any likeness of anything that is in the heaven above, or that is in the earth beneath, or that is in the water under the earth; you shall not bow down to them or serve them " (Ex. 20:4, 5).

Science enables us to soar into the heavens, to conquer the earth, and to penetrate the depths of the oceans, but it still is man-made. It must not be given the supreme devotion which belongs to God alone, and it must not be used like an air pump to inflate man into a rival of God. Actually, the greatness and importance and continued progress of science are better appreciated and more effectively supported when the true function of science as a tool is understood than when it is overinflated into a god and worshiped as the all-sufficient method of solving every human problem.

"DEMOCRACY IS THE MEASURE . . ."

As we have just seen, the word "scientific" has great authority among us. But the word "democratic" has even greater authority. If something is done "unscientifically," we feel that this is too bad because probably it will not be done so efficiently or successfully as it might be. But if something is done "undemocratically," we feel that it is *wrong* because it transgresses against the ideal of our American way of life.

What do we mean by "democracy"? Probably we think first of all of the Constitution, of the individual rights it guarantees and of the political institutions that have been set up so that these rights can be safeguarded. But democracy means much more than a method of making laws and carrying on governmental administration through the leadership of men and women elected by popular vote. Our political order provides the structure within which we are able to follow a "way of life" which we proudly call "democratic."

On its economic side we speak of this way of life as free enterprise; on its social side we speak of it as equality of opportunity. Translated into everyday language, freedom and equality mean that any person — by applying himself, by using the talents he has and the skills he acquires — can "get ahead" and rise from a lower to a higher position in society. The life of Abraham Lincoln has come to symbolize this meaning of

democracy for most of us. Lincoln was born a humble man of
the people, yet he also was a man who aspired to greatness and
who moved beyond the lower reaches of American society to
the highest level of power and prestige. He rose from log cabin
to White House. Free enterprise and equality of opportunity
provide the motive power for much of what we do in our daily
lives. Furthermore, they make us all partners in the well-being
of each other, for even when we are competing with one another to " get ahead," we feel that every person has a stake in
the common good.

Democracy goes even deeper, however, than these political,
economic, and social meanings. We share the conviction of our
American forefathers that our democracy represents a new beginning in human history, a noble experiment, a new order of
life different from and superior to anything achieved in the
past. Democracy means idealism. It involves being dissatisfied
with just making money or climbing the social ladder unless
these types of worldly success can be justified in higher
terms — such as " service " or " stewardship " or " the general
welfare." It involves feeling called to be true to the " American
dream." Woodrow Wilson once said: " Sometimes people call
me an idealist. Well, that is the way I know I'm an American:
America is the most idealistic nation in the world."

We believe in democracy, we are deeply loyal to it, and we
try to govern our living according to our understanding of
it. In other words, according to our definition of religion in
Chapter 1, democracy is a powerful religious factor in American life. The beliefs and standards we have described command such a quality of loyalty and give us such a strong sense
of " belonging together " that we might well call democracy
the " common religion " of our society.

Reinhold Niebuhr, as reported in *Time* magazine, made the
following observation a few years ago after he had heard and

read a large number of speeches delivered at college and high school graduation exercises: " If one may judge by the various commencement utterances, . . . Americans have only one religion: devotion to democracy. They extol its virtues, are apprehensive about the perils to which it is exposed, pour maledictions upon its foes, rededicate themselves periodically to its purposes, and claim unconditioned validity for its ideals. Does not the very extravagance of our devotion prove that we live in a religiously vapid age, in which even Christians fail to penetrate to the more ultimate issues of life? "

Did Dr. Niebuhr mean that if Christians " penetrate to the more ultimate issues of life " they will give up their devotion to democracy? Of course not. He meant that this devotion should be placed in proper position in the light of the deepest Christian devotion, which is supposed to be directed to God and his righteousness. He was challenging Christians to beware of making democracy the object of *supreme* loyalty in such a way as to transform it into a false god, an idol.

Is this a real danger? Usually it does not even occur to us that democracy might be a rival to Christian faith. How can democracy be a rival when the churches occupy a place of such great prestige in the American scheme of things? We are somewhat vague about the exact relationship, but we take for granted that democracy is an expression of Christian principles. Yet the relations between Christianity and democracy actually have been complicated rather than simple, and more often indirect than direct. Historians still are battling over the question whether or not the rise of democracy was dependent on Christianity, and the truth seems to be that our free society developed through the interaction of both Christian and non-Christian forces. Perhaps many of us identify Christianity and democracy with one another because we know more about democracy than we do about Christianity.

Such vagueness can lead to confusion. For example, what are we to say about the interest of many American leaders and groups in a "return to religion" or a "back to God" movement when we know that their concern has been aroused mainly by the Communist threat to the free world? This looks like a mobilization of religion in defense of democracy. Such a project may be proper, for Christians rightly love democracy. But it also may be idolatrous. The question is: Which is supreme in the situation, democracy or God? Which is serving which? If Christianity is prized because it provides an underpinning for freedom, individualism, and other important features of the democratic way of life, then God is being made the servant of democracy and democracy is being worshiped as though it were supreme. The time has come when we ought to sharpen our understanding in order to avoid confusion.

First, let us consider the place of the "official religions" (Protestant, Roman Catholic, Jewish) in American life. The most significant fact is that the democratic way of life provides the *setting* in which the various religious communities operate. It is like a big circus tent that overarches the three rings in which performances are given. Every American may exercise "freedom of religion," which means that he can join the activities in any one of the three rings of the major religions or he can ignore them if he so chooses. But even if he decides not to become "actively religious," he still remains under the "big top" of the democratic way of life.

This setup makes religious faith seem to be optional and simply a matter of individual taste. Test yourself. Would you say that it is more important to be a Protestant, Roman Catholic, or Jew than it is to be an American? You see, automatically we think of ourselves first of all as Americans, not as Christians or Jews. The very fact that our churches compete on the open market with any number of social and fraternal and service organizations for our time and support tends to make us feel that although church activity is a good thing it is not any more important than these other activities. Even the people who are devoted to the life of a church often seem to think of religion as a special room in the house of our democracy rather than as the electric system that gives light and power to the whole house.

The fact that the various religious communions operate within the setting of democracy opens the way for someone to come along and say: " Go ahead and be a member of a church if you want to, but remember that your first loyalty belongs to the democracy which gives you freedom to believe whatever you want to believe. After all, religion is a private matter. If you think that the faith of your church does you some good, that's fine. But so far as I am concerned, the real heart of democracy lies in the way you live with other people, and that's religion enough for me." This point of view makes the democratic way of life the object of a super faith that reduces Christian faith to secondary importance. Faith in democracy is accepted as an alternative to Christian faith in God.

Recently a study was made of the relation between what people say about religion and what they actually do in their everyday living. A majority of the large number of individuals who were questioned testified that they regarded religion as something " very important." Yet within a minute or two they answered other questions which showed that they did not think their religious beliefs had any real effect on their ideas or conduct in politics and business. What is going on here? *Some* ideas and standards actually govern these people in their business and political affairs. If they are not ideas and standards associated with the teachings of religion, what are they? Probably these persons are guided and supported by democracy — faith in the democratic way of life — which is their " working faith" even though they do not think of it in religious terms.

One important American who frankly believed that democracy should be the "common faith" of all Americans and who devoted much of his life to fostering such a faith was Professor John Dewey. Let us look for a moment at why and how he did it.

Professor Dewey was deeply concerned about the tremendous variety of languages, customs, beliefs, and religions among the millions of immigrants who were rapidly filling up our country during the early years of this century. He knew that all these people must somehow learn to live with one another peaceably and co-operatively in spite of many deep-seated differences. It seemed to him that the ideals and values of democracy offered a core around which all Americans could be united. He suggested that because devotion to democratic ideals need not be expressed in any formal pattern of worship, these ideals could be accepted wholeheartedly by everyone regardless of race, creed, color, or national origin. Therefore he advocated a "common faith" in the democratic way of life. He criticized the churches because he believed that they were fostering divisions among Americans. He urged them to function as agencies for the transmission of the "common faith," and predicted that unless they decided to do so they would be shoved into the background.

Professor Dewey was particularly interested in the public schools because he regarded them as the most effective means of promoting unity. He actually looked upon the task of the schools as fundamentally religious. Here are his own words: "Our schools, in bringing together those of different nationalities, languages, traditions, and creeds, in assimilating them together on the basis of what is common and public in endeavor and achievement, are performing an infinitely significant religious work. They are promoting the social unity out of which in the end genuine religious unity must grow."

The most striking feature of this project was Professor Dewey's expectation that it could be carried through successfully without any direct mention of religion. Religion must be kept out of the school curriculum and teachers must refrain from expressing their own religious convictions openly. Why? For fear that they would indoctrinate students with some particular version of the Judaeo-Christian tradition which would separate students from each other rather than unite them all in allegiance to a "common faith." In the meantime, democratic ideals and values should be held up as a proper object of loyalty, and school activities in the classroom and on the playground should give practical experience in the democratic way of life.

In place of religion in the traditional sense of doctrine and church, therefore, Professor Dewey advocated what he called a "religious attitude" toward democratic living. He was entirely correct in saying that Americans can be "religious" without being members of a church or a synagogue. He was defining religion as we have defined it: it isn't *what* a person believes but *how* he believes it that makes a belief religious. However, he was wrong in thinking that "being religious" about democracy would not add up to a full-fledged religion. Actually his "common faith" was an *alternative* to Christianity, a new civic religion designed to bind all Americans into one great people in a way that divided Christianity supposedly cannot.

Or perhaps it would be more accurate to say that Professor Dewey was not urging the *invention* of a new religion but merely urging us to discover what is going on beneath the surface of American life and to acknowledge openly the *real god* we serve.

Let us put the matter bluntly: Is our devotion to the democratic way of life a super faith which is more potent in our day-to-day living than our Christian faith? Do we give democracy the supreme loyalty that belongs to God alone? Many of us are bound to recoil violently against the suggestion that we might be doing any such thing. But let us ask some additional questions. Don't we often talk about the Christian faith as primarily a " way of life "? And what happens when we try to spell out what we mean by the Christian " way of life "? Don't we pretty much describe the democratic " way of life "? Precisely what have we Christians got that a sincere believer in Professor Dewey's " common faith " does not have? The obvious answer is, " Faith in God." Yet our understanding of God often is so vague that it is difficult for us to explain what we mean when we try to show that faith in God is important. Usually the argument boils down to " we *don't* need God " versus " we *do* need God." What do we Christians say?

We say something like this: Faith is deeper than " the way you live with other people." It has to do with the character of people themselves. This is true of democracy too. Democracy is not automatic. Democratic liberties and methods of procedure depend on *persons*. Democracy will not survive unless we pay attention to the character of the individuals who exercise these liberties and who follow these procedures. Ideals and values are fine, but there is a gap between knowing what is right and doing it. The gap must be bridged by character. What is the source of power that can help us to be the right kind of persons? We have some power of our own, but we need a " power additive." That is where faith in God comes in. Through faith we have access to God's power. Christianity makes us better persons, the kind of persons who are the true bulwark of democracy.

The shortcoming of this approach is that the center of concern remains with democracy. In effect, we are saying that democracy is the thing we really are most concerned about and that God is important as a means of getting what we want.

This is idolatry, and as we look at it, it becomes less and less convincing. We remember Professor Dewey, and we think of the great number of purely nominal Christians and nonchurch people who seem to have the power to practice the democratic virtues every bit as well or even better than some extremely active church members. So far as we can tell, they are honest, just, generous, sensitive, and outgoing in their relations with others. They do not feel the need for a " power additive." Where do we go from here?

Well, let us dig deeper. Let us get at the roots of democracy, the roots of freedom and equality. Take equality, for instance. The Declaration of Independence states that " all men are created equal," and as we have mentioned earlier, equality is acknowledged by all of us to be a cornerstone of our way of life. Yet we know that the phrase " all men are created equal " is by no means literally true. We are not born with equal abilities. We do not develop equally. More important, impartial study of American economic and social facts has shown that *all* Americans do not have equality of opportunity to " get ahead " or even equality before the law. Apparently, then, our belief in equality is rooted in a conviction that we hold in spite of experiences that contradict it. Where does it come from?

Will Herberg has answered directly and forcefully:

" American democracy is committed to the ideal and the ethics of equality. It sees no justification for any inequality in social life except and in so far as it is made necessary by the requirements of society, and even then inequality is regarded as at best a necessary evil. Ultimately, this radical claim to equality can be justified only by a belief in the essential equality of all men *in their relationship to God* — positively in their destiny as children of God, negatively as sinners before God, in whose sight no one can claim any pre-eminence over another. Every attempt to establish an equalitarian ethic in exclusively nonreligious, humanistic terms must fail, since aside from their God relationship there is literally nothing in which all men are 'created equal.' . . . [Persons] who reject our religious heritage, yet affirm human equality, are not only intellectually incoherent; they are, quite unwittingly, of course, engaged in destroying the roots of the values they themselves hold most precious."

This excellent statement suggests what might be called a "Christmas-tree approach" to understanding many of our neighbors who are "good, moral Americans" although they are indifferent or only lukewarm about Christian faith. These persons are dependent on the Judaeo-Christian tradition for basic convictions around which they organize their lives, while at the same time they have cut themselves off from the source of these convictions. Apparently they are convinced that democratic beliefs about the nature and purpose and meaning of life can live on indefinitely apart from communion with the living God in the light of whose revelation of himself these beliefs "make sense." Their beliefs are like the Christmas trees we bring into our homes every year. We can keep them alive for a while by putting their trunks in water or by treating them with chemicals, but we know that eventually they must die because they have been cut off from their roots.

Let us be quite clear about what we are saying here. We are not attacking personalities. We are not predicting that our neighbors are going to give up their beliefs and become traitors to democracy. In situations of storm and stress they may do so — but so may we. It is entirely possible for them to continue throughout their lifetime to adorn American life and to contribute to its integrity. We should be grateful for their presence and for their example. The question is whether *in the long run* democracy can feed upon itself, or whether it depends on beliefs that will continue to live and grow only if they are nourished by conscious commitment to the living God.

The heart of our difficulty lies in the fact that even our *conception of God* has been shaped more by the ideas and attitudes and desires of democracy than by the Bible and Christian tradition. We are not merely tempted to idolize democracy. We are tempted to make God himself into an idol by fitting him in with our way of life.

About ten years ago a Jewish rabbi, Joshua Loth Liebman, wrote a book which he gave the title *Peace of Mind*. This book surprised both its author and its publisher by rapidly becoming a best seller. Perhaps the title alone accounted for many sales. But the wide attention it has received through the years shows that Rabbi Liebman's approach to religion appeals to a great many people, regardless of their denomination. One reason lies in the assurance the book offers that modern scientific psychology has discovered new answers to the age-old problems of conscience, love, fear, grief, and God. Another lies in the assurance that psychology brings "encouraging news from the scientific clinic about man's infinite capacity to change and improve himself" (p. xiv). This is news that all of us appreciate because it reinforces our characteristic democratic virtues of optimism, initiative, self-confidence, and self-reliance.

The heart of the book, however, is a section in which Rabbi Liebman introduces "A New God Idea for America." He insists that if we are to take advantage of the encouraging discoveries of psychology, we must give up our old ideas about God. Why? Because the traditional conception of God is "out of tune" with our contemporary life. We must construct a new idea "that will reflect America's democratic experience and culture." In fact, we Americans have a world-wide religious mission to perform, because " it will be from the democratic experience of our century that mankind will first learn its true dignity as independent and necessary partners to God."

Let us follow the rabbi's argument closely. He writes:

" The story of the human race, until the age of technological democracy, has really been the story of dependence and helplessness — of men really feeling impotent in the presence of poverty and disease, of tyranny and autocracy, before which they had to bow their heads in resignation. . . .

" America is different from Europe. In Europe the emphasis was too often upon obedience and dependence upon some strong power to whose will man had to submit. In America, . . . the emphasis has been upon self-reliance, upon every new generation doing better than its fathers, on becoming more successful in human attainments. One of the great troubles is that in our religion we have continued to picture our relationships to God in terms of the helpless, poverty-stricken, powerless motifs in European culture. Now, a religion that will emphasize man's nothingness and God's omnipotence; that calls upon us to deny our own powers and to glorify His — that religion may have fitted the needs of many Europeans, but it will not satisfy the growing self-confident character of America. . . .

" We must be brave enough to declare that every culture must create its own God idea rather than rely upon outworn tradition. . . . America must emphasize independence and interdependence. It should come to its God idea not through a feeling of helplessness, but through a feeling of confidence. . . . The religion of the future, for the first time, may become a partnership religion in which men will not only *say,* but will *feel,* that they are indispensable to God."

This is an exciting and inspiring vision. It is also amazingly convincing. And the reason it is so convincing is that what Rabbi Liebman pictures as a future achievement is actually a present reality among a great many of us Protestant Christians. We already worship a kindly, co-operative "senior partner God" and it makes us feel good to be assured by modern psychology and enlightened religion that we are on the right track. Is it not striking that a Jewish rabbi, speaking as an American to fellow Americans, can cut across denominational lines and advocate the kind of religion many of us think is *Christian* faith?

Rabbi Liebman's "New God Idea for America" is an open invitation to idolatry. We are to let our democratic culture tell us what we are like, and then we are to make God in our own image. From the standpoint of God's revelation of himself through the Biblical and Christian tradition, such a program rests squarely on not allowing God really to be God, and on setting up ourselves and the "way of life" we have created as the object of supreme loyalty. Certainly it is true that we are bound to think of God in terms of our own experience. We cannot jump out of our own skins. If God confronts us in the midst of our daily living, and if our daily living takes place in a democratic culture, then it is inevitable that we shall think of God as related to democracy. But note this: God as *related to* democracy, not God as *defined by* democracy. The difference may not seem great on the surface, but the whole issue of idolatry versus true faith is expressed in the difference between these two phrases.

God as related to democracy makes room for us to acknowledge God as the *Lord* of democracy, as he is the Lord of all men and all societies. God as *defined by* democracy limits God; it denies God's freedom and sovereignty and looks upon God as the *servant* of democracy. The very idea that we Americans and our way of life are indispensable to God is idolatrous and blasphemous. How could we ever get such a notion unless we assumed that we were sitting on the throne of God and understood all mysteries and all knowledge?

How can we avoid making democracy a big idol and God a " senior partner idol " which supports our big idol? At the very least we must stop thinking of democracy as the circus tent that overarches every aspect of our lives. And in order to do this we must recognize God as the all-encompassing reality in whom we live and move and have our being. And in order to do this, we must first of all be confronted by God as he has revealed himself in Biblical and Christian history.

The Biblical and Christian tradition teaches us that God has revealed himself as the One who *defines himself!* The clear implication is that when God reveals himself to us today he comes to us from beyond democracy. We are to serve God in and through our democratic way of life, *but* we are to live with a constant awareness that the final meaning of our life is rooted and grounded in God and not in American democracy. Furthermore, the Biblical and Christian tradition teaches us that God has revealed himself as the One who *defines us!* Our democratic culture may tell us that the secret of our human nature is " our infinite capacity to improve ourselves." But we Christians should know that no matter what picture of ourselves we get from our culture, this picture is subject to criticism and correction in the light of God's Word. The Christian faith involves a point of view that is independent of democracy, a point of view that is never to be whittled down to fit neatly into a place — even a very honored place — in the democratic scheme of things.

"THE NATION IS THE MEASURE . . ."

Here is a paragraph from a letter written recently by a minister of a church in northern Ohio:

"An American legionnaire absolutely refuses to come to church now that we have voted that in the sanctuary our flags will be placed so that the position of honor is occupied by the Christian flag instead of the American flag. . . . Along the same line, let me tell you about our early service on the third of July. It is customary for the congregation to remain seated during the singing of the second hymn. Well, I just about had a rebellion on my hands because I did not ask the people to stand up this time. The hymn was 'America the Beautiful.' It's perfectly all right, apparently, to sit down for 'Our God, Our Help in Ages Past' but irreverent to do so when we sing about our nation. Incidentally, I have noticed for a number of years that congregations sing patriotic hymns with more spirit than almost any other hymns. Even men and women who usually don't sing at all join in. Is this because these songs are so much better known than any others? I don't think so. It is because our nation is a very real object of love and devotion while God seems vague and unreal. When we sing a patriotic hymn the feeling surges through us that we belong to something great and powerful, but when we sing about God or Christ or the Church we aren't so sure."

This letter points to one of the most perplexing religious developments in modern times — the tendency of patriotism to become nationalistic and idolatrous. Today every man is supposed to place his nation above every interest and to love his country to the point of sacrificing his life for it. This is the one supreme loyalty that practically all men acknowledge and obey.

The claim of nations to supreme loyalty is so powerful today that even movements like science and democracy, whose basic convictions and goals rise above the division of mankind into nation-states, have been narrowed down and identified with national interest. For example: until recently it was taken for granted that achievements of scientists anywhere belonged to scientists everywhere, and to all the peoples of the world. Now the greatest discoveries, especially those which have to do with atomic energy, are monopolized by Governments which subsidize further research as part of their national defense system. Or think of democracy: it used to be taken for granted that democratic freedoms and rights belonged to all men and that before long they would be achieved everywhere. Yet today we Americans do not consider democracy an international movement as often as we look upon it as an American achievement that makes our nation different from other nations and superior to them. Democracy means the United States, and the United States is the greatest nation on the face of the earth. Democracy is *our* patented trade-mark.

Thus in a time of tension and insecurity the "one world" implications of science and democracy have been pushed into the background and subordinated to concern for the nation.

Of course nationalism has affected Communism too. It is

very significant that during the Second World War, Stalin did not unite the Russian people under the banner of international Communism as he should have in accordance with the true doctrine of the Communist movement. He appealed to love of Mother Russia. At the end of the war he decreed that the victory over Hitler would be commemorated forever as " The Great Patriotic War, 1941–1945." In recent years Russian policy obviously has been guided by the motto " Russia First." So far as science is concerned, the Russians long since have denied that international co-operation of scientists helped the rapid progress of modern science. Instead they claim that every major discovery was made by a Russian! This is national self-glorification carried to a ridiculous extreme. We should add that Jugoslavian Communism also is intensely nationalistic and that the Chinese Communists likewise operate on the basis of superpatriotic appeals.

In every part of the world there are individuals and groups who fan the flame of nationalistic loyalty in the belief that only in this way can they " save the nation " or " keep the nation strong." They are painfully sensitive about "national sovereignty" and attack any suggestion that their nation does not have the right to be a law unto itself. They are vigilantly suspicious of any citizen who is " too critical " about national policies or attitudes because it seems to them that criticism of any kind betrays a lack of the " all out " loyalty every " true " citizen must have.

Even on purely political grounds, therefore, nationalism is dangerous. It rigidly defends the nation *as it is,* and too much rigidity can result in *rigor mortis.* At its best, nationalism proudly overestimates the power and wisdom and virtue any one nation possesses in comparison with other nations. At its worst, nationalism invites nations to behave in an utterly selfish and irresponsible way in a world whose future depends on willingness to enter into responsible relationships with other nations.

But we are especially concerned about the religious implications of our native form of nationalism, which we are going to call "Americanism." By "Americanism" we mean that type of belief which regards the United States as the supreme value, as the source of life's meaning, as an end-in-itself and a law-unto-itself. We mean that type of devotion which seeks to persuade individuals and organizations to make the might and glory and above all the security of the United States their chief aim in life. There is nobility in such devotion, as there is in any commitment to a cause greater than ourselves that delivers us from bondage to self-centeredness. But the "catch" in super-patriotism is that it does not really overcome self-centeredness. Americanism offers us an opportunity to feel important and proud and powerful in a way that feeds our self-centeredness and our craving to be significant. It is a kind of extended self-centeredness. We join together to swell the chorus of praise to the greatness of America, and then each of us says to himself: "Think of it! *I* am an American!" The greater we think America is, the greater we feel we are as individuals, and in making an idol of our nation we secretly idolize ourselves.

The tendency to put the nation above everything else makes a powerful impact on the moral judgments of Americans, even on the judgments of persons who are not consciously or actively superpatriotic. This impact can be seen in the results of a poll reported in the *Ladies' Home Journal*. The persons interviewed were asked to look within themselves and to state honestly whether they thought they really obeyed the law of love under certain special conditions. When the results were tabulated they looked like this:

1. Do you love persons belonging to a different religion?
   90% said yes; 5% said no.

2. Do you love members of another race?
    80% said yes; 12% said no.

3. Do you love your business competitors?
    78% said yes; 10% said no.

But now comes a sudden shift. Note the change carefully.

4. Do you love members of a political party that you think
    is dangerous? (Obviously the Communist Party was im-
    plied in this question.)
    27% said yes; 57% *said no.*

5. Do you love enemies of this nation?
    25% said yes; 63% *said no.*

These figures tell us that generally speaking most of us feel
we ought to " love our neighbor " in spite of differences of race
or creed or business interest, *but* a majority of us are quite
ready to throw Christian love overboard as soon as the situation involves loyalty to our nation or the security of our nation.

Christian faith includes the demand not only that we " love
our neighbors " but also that we " love our enemies." If devotion to our country authorizes us to hate " subversives " and
outside enemies with a clear conscience, we certainly have a
conflict of loyalties on our hands. There is no doubt that such
a conflict rages within many of us again and again.

Yet there is no doubt that there also are many of us who do
not feel any tension at all between loyalty to God and loyalty
to our country. Why is this the case? Perhaps the reason is
that we simply have not faced up to the problem. But another
possibility is that we sincerely identify the will of God with the
will of the United States. This is an especially subtle temptation for us in the present anxiety-producing world situation.
Communism so obviously represents an evil, tyrannical power
that we are certain God must be against it. We are against it
too. Therefore it would seem that God's will and our nation's

will are one and the same. Bosley Crowther of *The New York Times* wrote a review of a movie based on the Korean War in which he remarked that according to the vast majority of Americans there are only two areas in which it really makes a difference what one believes: (1) every American must detest Communism as atheistic, devilish, totally false, and un-American; and (2) every American must believe in this nation so completely that he will unquestioningly lay down his life for it when he is called upon to do so. Is it not true that many of us Christians agree with these beliefs because we believe that God is on our side and that in opposing Communism we are in some sense fighting God's battle?

Can we seriously entertain the thought that God may be against the United States too? As we continue to pull down our " barns " and build larger ones to store our surpluses and to pile up our atomic weapons, are we ever haunted by the realization that God might confront our country with the terrible words addressed to the rich man in Jesus' parable: " Fool! This night your soul is required of you; and the things you have prepared, whose will they be? " (Luke 12:20.) These are absolutely crucial questions for Christians. If we disregard them or passionately reject them, then Americanism has engulfed our religious life. Whatever may be the quality of devotion we think we give to God, actually we believe that America comes first. We are making an idol of our nation.

At this point we may be able to appreciate the astonishing up-to-dateness of the prophets of Israel, who prepared the way for Christianity by challenging the tendency of their people to identify God with the nation. They spoke in the name of a holy God who would not allow men to claim that he was " their God " more than he was the God of other nations. They prophesied that judgment and destruction would overtake every nation that exalted itself as the be-all and end-all of men's lives — *even if that nation were Israel!*

The letter that was quoted at the beginning of this chapter mentioned two flags. Why is the Christian flag supposed to be given a position of honor above the American flag? The reason is that the Christian flag stands for the supremacy of God over all men and all nations. The United States is not the final truth in terms of which Christians are to make their judgments and to live their lives. To paraphrase Shakespeare: " All the world's a stage, and all the many nations merely players. They strut and fret their hour upon the stage and then are heard no more." We hope and trust that the United States will not merely " strut and fret," and that the hour of human history in which our country plays its part will be a very long hour, but above and beyond any number of the " American Centuries " so dear to the heart of *Life* magazine lies the mysterious eternal creativity of God.

Among all Americans, the Christian should be the person whose fundamental standard of judgment is not the aspirations of the nation but the obligations of a faith in God which is both universal in its outreach and immediately personal in its application. Difficult though it may be, Christians must become sensitive to the fact that Americanism and Christianity are not facets of the same truth. To say " Christian faith " means, " This nation under God." To say " Americanism " means that the nation comes first, and this implies, " My nation, thou art my god." The greatest service Christians can render our country is to become actively concerned about the distinctive community and destiny of the Church *over against* American society. Churches should not be thought of merely as a natural, normal part of the American landscape. Churches are " colonies of heaven," which does not mean that they are " choirs of angels " but rather that they are groups of people who take seriously the command: " Seek first his [God's] kingdom and his righteousness, and all these things [including the things that belong to the life of the nation] shall be yours as well " (Matt. 6:33). If Christians are faithful and if the Church is the Church, there is bound to be tension — creative tension — between Christianity and our national life which grows out of constant awareness that the Kingdom of God is never to be identified with the kingdoms of this world, not even with " America the Beautiful."

What have we learned in these three chapters on " secret gods "?

1. Christian faith does not demand that we cast doubt on the validity of science as a way of controlling our environment, or that we belittle the virtue of democracy as a method of political and social organization, or that we deny the importance of patriotism as a means of fostering unity in our nation. But Christian faith does demand that no human power or program or movement or community shall be overinflated into a " god " which claims our last full measure of devotion. Some Americans actually substitute one or more of these ingredients of our way of life for God. Others become confused and divided in their religious loyalties because they are not keenly aware of the danger of idolatry. We cannot understand the dynamics of the religious situation in our country unless we go behind the statistics and look at the loyalties that really grasp people effectively and shape their attitudes and their decisions.

2. Science, democracy, and patriotism are the most significant and the most tempting social idols of our day for two reasons:

a. The very greatness and success of these enterprises make it easy for us to put our trust in them rather than in God. Pride in the greatness of our achievements makes us feel self-sufficient and equal to meeting the requirements of the good life through our modern scientific techniques, our democratic institutions, and our national power.

b. On the other hand, we are living in a " time of troubles " when many of the old foundations seem to be disintegrating and when large numbers of us feel terribly insecure in spite of our outward appearance of power and prosperity. Despair in the face of insecurity tempts us to give ourselves with frantic and absolute devotion to " practical " scientific, democratic, or nationalistic programs because they seem to offer escape from futility. The " secret gods " appeal to our pride and to our despair. Actually, pride and despair are opposite sides of the same coin, and the coin itself we have called idolatry.

3. American Christianity must bear much of the responsibility for the widespread worship of these idols. Many of us Christians and our churches feel entirely too much " at home " inside American society. We have soft-pedaled the necessity of distinguishing between Christianity and American culture. We have evaded the implications of Christ's demand that Christians are supposed to be *in* the world but not *of* it. All too often we dance to the tune of the world around us, rearranging the elements of our faith to make them blend harmoniously with the music of the American way of life. No wonder some of our neighbors feel that there is nothing distinctive about Christian faith and decide to give their allegiance directly to such concerns as science, democracy, and nationalism which obviously exert a powerful influence on the affairs of everyday life.

The conclusion to which our detective work brings us, therefore, is that the nature and meaning of Christian faith cannot be taken for granted. Christians need to rediscover the distinctiveness of Christianity as the one and only true alternative to idolatry.

CHAPTER

5

THE "RETURN TO RELIGION"

Religion is making the headlines today, and no Protestant leaders have been making more of them than Rev. Norman Vincent Peale and Rev. Billy Graham. Both men have been tremendously popular, and the general public has thought of them as spearheading America's impressive "return to religion." The teachings of Norman Vincent Peale and Billy Graham are worth particular study not alone in connection with their public careers, which like everyone's must be temporary; but, more important, because they represent persistently popular interpretations of Christianity.

Certainly Christians should be thankful that many people are being reached who have been lukewarm in their religious commitment or who have been indifferent to Christianity. But our survey of secret gods indicates that the recent upswing in religious interest should not be accepted at face value. For instance, do Norman Vincent Peale and Billy Graham recognize the tendencies toward idolizing science, democracy, and the nation which complicate and confuse the present religious situation? Do they attack our idolatries or do they unwittingly encourage the kind of undiscriminating approach that leaves the idols undisturbed?

First let us look carefully at the message of Norman Vincent

Peale from the point of view of idolatry. One feature of Dr. Peale's approach is that he concentrates his attention so exclusively on problems of personal living that he does not very often touch on the life of groups. He gives little indication of being aware of devotion to democracy or to " America the Beautiful " as rivals to devotion to God. However, when it comes to science and the success that science makes possible, the approach of Dr. Peale is quite clear. He enthusiastically supports the modern cult of the practical and the technical. In fact, he interprets religion itself " scientifically " in terms of " know-how " and " getting results." One theme is repeated endlessly throughout all his preaching and writing: *You* can overcome all difficulties and achieve whatever you want to achieve if you will only realize that " religious faith is not something piously stuffy but is a scientific procedure for successful living." In other words, faith is a sure-fire technique for getting what you want out of life. If the true-story illustrations Dr. Peale sprinkles lavishly over almost every page of his famous best seller, *The Power of Positive Thinking,* are any indication, the type of faith he advertises can guarantee happiness, prosperity, friends, peace of mind, boundless energy, self-confidence, and health. No wonder so many people are interested.

The secret of human nature, according to Dr. Peale, is that " *as you think, so shall you be.*" He writes:

" In the last analysis the basic reason a person fails to live a creative and successful life is because of error within himself. He thinks wrong. He needs to correct the error in his thoughts. . . .

" You can think your way to failure and unhappiness, but you can also think your way to success and happiness. The world in which you live is not primarily determined by outward conditions and circumstances but by thoughts that habitually occupy your mind. . . . To change your circumstances, first start thinking differently. Do not passively accept unsatisfactory circumstances, but form a picture in your mind of circumstances as they should be. Hold that picture, develop it firmly in all details, believe in it, pray about it, work at it, and you can actualize it according to that mental image emphasized in your positive thinking. . . .

"If you think in negative terms, you will get negative results. If you think in positive terms, you will achieve positive results. That is the simple fact which is at the basis of an astonishing law of prosperity and success."

In line with this " thought control " approach, Dr. Peale defines religion as " a system of thought discipline." Religion consists of rules and procedures that enable a person to achieve success, prosperity, and happiness by thinking positively rather than negatively.

An elementary knowledge of psychology plus a little common sense will tell us that *some* situations and social relations actually can be affected by positive or negative attitudes. A minister arrived at a Women's Guild meeting " feelin' mighty low," and when he responded to the greeting of the hostess with the words, " Oh, I'm all right, I guess," she chided him and said: " Don't be so negative. Always say that you are feeling fine." So as he went from group to group the minister kept telling the ladies that he was " feeling fine " — and pretty soon he *was!* But, as he said in a sermon a few Sundays later, " What has this sort of thing to do with the Christian faith? " An elementary knowledge of the Bible and Christian tradition plus a little common sense will tell us that if we deal with experiences of being tense, unloved, lonely, fearful, purposeless, and unsuccessful by refusing to think about them and by stuffing our minds with " positive thoughts " of sweetness and light, we cut ourselves off from any deep and honest under-standing of ourselves and of our relation to God, in whose pres-ence we are supposed to see ourselves as we really are.

Almost invariably Dr. Peale speaks of God in completely " positive " terms. When he writes about God's relationship to men in person-to-person language, he advises his readers that " another effective technique in problem solving is the simple device of conceiving of God as a partner. . . . Christianity teaches that in all the difficulties, problems, and circumstances of this life God is close by. We can talk to him, lean upon him, get help from him, and have the inestimable benefit of his in-terest, support, and help. Practically everybody believes in a general way that this is true, and many have experienced the reality of this faith."

Certainly it is comforting to think of God as a " partner " who continually is backing up one's efforts to achieve success and prosperity and happiness. But this is an overfamiliar and dangerously one-sided interpretation of *who God is*. He has re-vealed himself in the Biblical story, not primarily as our part-ner, but as our Lord and Savior — who also is our Judge.

The most disquieting feature of Dr. Peale's message, how-ever, is the fact that usually he speaks of God as a source of power which we can channel into ourselves by using the proper techniques. He says that just as there exist scientific techniques for the release of atomic energy, so there are scientific proce-dures for the release of spiritual energy through the *mecha-nism* of prayer. Prayer is a vital part of the " power-releasing process " by which " individuals can tap forces and utilize strength not otherwise available." Since prayer is not so much a person-to-person relationship to God as it is a mechanism, Dr. Peale quite logically tells us that " it is well to study prayer from an efficiency point of view." After all, in business and in-dustry the scientific way of testing methods and procedures is to find out how efficiently they produce results. Prayer involves methods and procedures too, and Dr. Peale concludes that any method that gets results — or as he puts it, " any method that stimulates the power of God to flow into the mind " — is legitimate and usable.

Just as there are authoritative scientific textbooks that list formulas which have been tested and proved, so there is a " prayer textbook " which guarantees successful results provided its formulas are followed closely. This, of course, is the Bible. Says Dr. Peale, " The most powerful force in human nature is the spiritual-power technique taught in the Bible." How is the Bible to be used as a textbook of spiritual science? Here is an example:

Two " famous industrialists " were facing a difficult business and technical problem. They believed that in dealing with prayer as a phenomenon they should " scrupulously follow the formulas outlined in the Bible." They selected these three " formulas ":

1. " According to your faith be it done to you." (Matt. 9:29.)

2. " Whatever you ask in prayer, believe that you receive it, and you will." (Mark 11:24.)

3. " If two of you agree on earth about anything they ask, it will be done for them by my Father in heaven." (Matt. 18:19.)

The two men prayed, affirming over and over again that they would be successful, and allowing no " negative " thought of failure to enter their minds. They were unsuccessful. So they decided to try an additional " formula." Verse 20 of Matt., ch. 18, reads:

4. " Where two or three are gathered in my name, there am I in the midst of them."

One of the men called in a country preacher friend of his and the *three* men prayed together. This time the outcome was satisfactory. Later the men said: "While we cannot explain it, the fact remains that we were baffled by our problem and we tried prayer according to the formulas of the New Testament. The method worked and we got a beautiful result."

Such a conversion of the Bible into a source book of "scientific" formulas for getting what we want is utterly blasphemous. It is neither authentic science nor authentic Christian faith. *It is magic.* Such prayer is built on the outrageous assumption that we can manipulate God for our own purposes just as we manipulate steam and electricity and atomic energy for our purposes. It reduces God to a vast reservoir of obedient power which we can control more and more efficiently as we learn the proper techniques.

Furthermore, Dr. Peale completely overlooks the fact that the fellowship with God pictured in the Bible *as a whole* involves bringing our darkest negative thoughts and actions out into the open *precisely when we pray.* Think of the desperate prayers in many of the psalms, Jeremiah's "negative" prayers, the confessions of Jesus' disciples concerning their weakness and sinfulness, the "unsuccessful" prayers of the apostle Paul regarding a physical disability he wanted removed, the prayer of Christ himself in the Garden of Gethsemane. Here we find a frank, honest, painful facing of *all* the facts of life. We find failure as well as success, weakness as well as power, doubt as well as faith, despair as well as hope, fear as well as confidence. Far from teaching that we should never "use a negative thought in prayer," the Bible brands unwillingness to open ourselves completely to God's "negative criticism" as rebellion against God and idolatrous worship of ourselves. According to the over-all message of the Bible and Christian tradition, peace, power, and victorious living arise out of an acceptance of our real limitations (which Dr. Peale tempts us to deny) and out of repeated confession that our wants and wishes are confused, misdirected, and infected with selfishness (which Dr. Peale tempts us to ignore).

The overwhelming impression Dr. Peale leaves with us is that we are not really to take no for an answer. Over and over again he assures us that positive thinking *gets results*. In the very same chapter in which he talks about bringing our desires under the scrutiny of God, he goes right on to say, " Every day as you confront the problems of life, I suggest that you affirm as follows: ' I believe God gives me power to attain what I really want.' " The primary emphasis in his message is on *our* power to get hold of God's power. *The Power of Positive Thinking* is crammed with " confidence-concepts," " faith-attitudes," " energy-producing thoughts," " spirit-lifters," 10 simple workable rules for developing confidence, 8 practical formulas for gaining an untroubled mind, 3 proven secrets for keeping up our vigor, 4 words that lead to success, and 7 simple steps for releasing creative mind power, plus innumerable other recommendations concerning the " scientific procedures " by which we can overcome all obstacles and gain our heart's desire.

In spite of our respect for Norman Vincent Peale's sincerity, and in spite of our respect for the persons who are attracted by his message, we are bound to wonder whether it is God in whom we are to trust or whether we are to rely mainly on ourselves and on our ability to practice Dr. Peale's magical " positive thinking."

From the point of view of idolatry, certain conclusions are clear. Dr. Peale's message is dominated by the success religion of our modern culture. It encourages and supports the idolatrous confidence that scientific ingenuity and scientific know-how can enable us to solve all our problems. His cult of " positive thinking " puts *man* in the driver's seat instead of God, and broadcasts the good news that we are to work out our own salvation, not with reverence and humility, but with confidence and efficiency. Norman Vincent Peale does not challenge our secret gods. He either ignores them or he sanctions them and clothes them with tattered remnants of the Christian faith.

In contrast to Dr. Peale, Billy Graham knows something about idols and does not hesitate to attack them. Here are three brief paragaphs that illustrate his approach:

"Look around you right this minute. At this very moment in history you see in America a country that has political freedom to an extent that is undreamed of in many parts of the civilized world. You see the greatest and most far-reaching public education system that man has ever created, and we are eulogized at home and abroad for our high standard of living. 'The American way of life' we like to call this fully electrified, fully automatic, chrome-plated economy of ours — but has it made us happy? Has it brought us the joy and satisfaction and the reason for living that we were seeking?

"No. As we stand here feeling smug and proud that we have accomplished so much that generations before us only dreamed about; as we span our oceans in hours instead of months; as we produce miracle drugs that wipe out some of man's most dread diseases; as we erect buildings that make the Tower of Babel seem an anthill; as we learn more and more of the mysterious secrets that lie in the depths of the sea, and peer further and further into outer space, do we lose one iota of that empty feeling within us? Do all these modern wonders bring us a sense of fulfillment, do they help to explain why we are here, do they point out what we are supposed to learn? . . .

"Let me tell you *where* we are and *what* we are. We are a

nation of empty people. . . . We have tried to fill ourselves
with science and education, with better living and pleasure,
with the many things we thought we wanted, but we are still
empty. Why are we empty? Because the Creator made us for
himself; and we shall never find completeness and fullness
apart from fellowship with him."

The theme of Billy Graham's message is not "positive thinking" but repentance. And when he calls us to repentance he
means that we are to *renounce* the idolatrous loyalties which
disintegrate our lives. He claims that political freedom and
education and high standard of living and all the other familiar ingredients of the American way of life are great
achievements, but that they are not saving things and that we
are damned if we put our faith and trust in them.

Billy Graham can make this "negative" message powerful
and popular because he is glamorous. Completely assured,
handsome in profile, vibrant and magnetic, he is a man who
obviously is equipped to "make something of himself" in the
personality cult of American success. He is just the kind of person Norman Vincent Peale tells us we can become. But what
does Billy Graham tell us? He tells us that he has renounced
the "success" cult in the name of Christian faith. As Donald
Meyer has pointed out, precisely because Graham is "slim and
gleaming" he gives many people the courage to renounce "the
impossible vision of salvation portrayed in the beautiful, full-
color advertisements" where life is always optimistic and
prosperous and happy and exciting and comfortable. Real life
isn't that way, and Billy Graham urges his listeners to have
nerve enough not to imagine that it can be that way. He offers
a salvation that puts a genuine but limited value on the science,
democracy, high standard of living, and success which Americans are tempted to substitute for the one true God.

Studied in the light of the great need for a Christian declaration of independence from the modern idols that confuse and divide our loyalties, Billy Graham's crusade for " peace with God " rather than " peace of mind " is very significant. This man is more than a Bible Belt evangelist who is putting on bigger and better revival meetings of a type that many of us staid Protestants react against. He is more than a literal-minded, narrow interpreter of the Bible of a type that many of us sophisticated and liberal Protestants react against. He is communicating the important insight that Christians must disengage themselves from the control of interests and concerns and loyalties which have become so much a part of the American scheme of things that the danger of their being false gods is difficult to see and even more difficult to face. He is preaching a prophetic " word " that needs to be heard.

Having said this, however, we must go on to point out that there are certain elements in Billy Graham's pattern which weaken his attack on idolatry.

For instance, he does not seem to realize the fact that his message involves a direct attack on Norman Vincent Peale's " positive thinking." He has emphasized the work of Dr. Peale with obvious approval. This is a distressing example of what can only be called a lack of discrimination. Apparently Billy Graham does not understand the cutting edge of his own insights.

Another weakness lies in the fact that he concentrates attention on personal, individual idolatry and ignores the subtle and widespread danger of group idolatries, especially the idolatry of nationalism. In spite of the fact that his Biblically centered approach gives him a basis for challenging our national self-worship, Graham continually thinks only in terms of changing individuals. When he talks about the nation the subject almost always is the struggle against Communism, which he calls "Satan's religion," and he suggests that we can be sure that God is on our side because we are opposing the Communists. He does not call for disengagement from proud and self-righteous "Americanism." He does not see that nothing in our present religious situation needs more criticism than our particular American combination of nationalism with popular Christianity.

Finally, Billy Graham seems to share with most of us American Protestants a naïve ignorance of the fact that the crucial battlefield on which the conflict between the true God and the false gods is being fought year by year and generation by generation is the life of the Christian Church — the life of faith itself.

Undoubtedly we are witnessing a "return to religion" in our generation. The question is: return to *what* religion? What is going on in the churches to which people are "returning"? What is happening "inside Christianity," where it is precisely Christian believers who face the most subtle temptation of all — the temptation to clothe the worship of something less than God in the garments of the Christian faith? Is there real debate and inner struggle among Christians in the churches concerning the nature and meaning of the Christian faith?

Until this dimension of the problem of idolatry is brought out into the open and faced squarely, we shall continually be short-circuiting our attempts to stand up to the idolatrous distortions of science, democracy, and patriotism that have infected American culture and American Christianity.

THE PROTESTANT REFORMERS AND "CHRISTIAN IDOLATRY"

Protestants ought to be especially sensitive to the danger of worshiping idols because Protestant Christianity was born out of a terrific battle within the Church over idolatry. Luther and Calvin charged that Christianity had become infected with idolatry, and they were very clear about what they meant by this accusation. Their analysis went something like this:

Whatever else Christian faith may be, basically it is a relationship between God and man. This relationship makes possible two types of faith — God-centered or man-centered. Christians always have been aware of God's centrality, but this awareness is not necessarily dominant in a person's actual living. A Christian may readily admit that God should be the center of his existence without realizing or accepting all that this implies. How can he know whether or not the controlling center of his religious life is on the side of God rather than on his own side?

Luther and Calvin believed that honest answers to two questions would indicate the true center of a person's faith:

1. Do you seek God because faith will benefit you?

2. Do you believe that sincere moral and religious effort can build the kind of relationship to God which will bring you these benefits?

They claimed the Roman Catholic Church of their time

had succumbed to the fatal temptation of encouraging Christians to answer yes to both of these questions. They asserted that, in effect, the Church said to people: " As a human being you have certain basic needs. The most important need is that you come into right relationship with God, for in union with God lies your eternal happiness. You must realize that it is to your interest to satisfy this need. God has established the Church to help you do that. You need help because God is utterly righteous and in order to win acceptance with him you must become good enough to merit fellowship with God. Now, what does the Church do for you? It starts you on your way through the sacrament of Baptism, which washes you clean. However, you will make mistakes and get off the track, so through confession and the discipline of penance, and through the guidance of the priest who is your spiritual father, the Church aids you in your growth. If you work hard and rely on the resources which the Church adds to your effort, eventually you will become worthy of God's approval. Then you will have satisfied your deepest need, and happiness — eternal happiness — will be yours."

The Reformers attacked this elaborate system because they believed that it made man — man's need and man's effort to qualify himself for having his need met — the center of Christian faith. They charged that any religion which promises a person that he will get out of his faith what he puts into it is essentially an appeal to self-centeredness. *And self-centeredness is the root of all idolatry.*

Luther himself began with a self-centered faith. He thought that his main problem was to achieve such complete obedience to God's law that he could be sure of God's favor and finally win the peace of mind he wanted so desperately. For years he " put in " everything that he had without " getting back " the bonus he expected. Then a " break-through " occurred in his inner life, sparked by intensive meditation upon the Scriptures and especially upon the letters of Paul. God brought Luther to realize that actually he had been worshiping himself. The more he had tried to get God on his side the more self-centered he became and the less God could mean to him.

Luther discovered that God was the opposite of his self-centeredness. He recognized the fact that a true relationship to God was not a matter of Martin Luther's needs or his desire for peace of mind, but rather a matter of acknowledging God and trusting God even if his own dearest desires were *not* fulfilled. This led him to define " salvation " as the realization of God's will and purpose — whatever that might be — rather than the satisfaction of human need. He went so far as to say that those who truly love God " freely offer themselves to all the will of God, even to hell and death eternally, should God so will, in order that his will may be fully done." Calvinist Protestants made the same point when they said that the Christian should be willing to be damned for the glory of God.

What was at stake here? Why did these people make such extreme statements, statements that seem terribly grim to us? *Luther and the Calvinists simply were trying to leave no loophole for man-centered faith.* They were utterly certain that we must affirm God without demanding that God affirm us, because only this type of faith can overcome the idolatry of self-centeredness. After all, what is the alternative? Shall we affirm God only in so far as he does what we want? Is God wise only if he agrees with us, good only if he makes us his favorites, and generous only if he charms away our suffering? True Christian faith means having confidence in God regardless of profit or loss. If we are not willing to love God unless we get something out of it for ourselves, we are secretly making ourselves the center rather than God. *Only those go to heaven who are willing not to go.* As Jesus said, " The man who tries to save his life will lose it; it is the man who loses his life for my sake and the Gospel's who will save it." (Mark 8:35, Phillips' translation.)

God is greater than the Christian religion; he is not tied to Christianity as men practice it. Whenever Christianity becomes man-centered, *God is opposed to it!* Therefore in the name of God, Luther and Calvin called for a revolutionary change-over to God-centeredness in Christian belief, worship, prayer, and in every activity connected with the life of faith.

Take prayer, for instance. Luther pointed out that we can pray the Lord's Prayer either "forward" or "backward." When we follow the order given by Jesus, we pray first of all for the praise of God, the coming of God's Kingdom, and the doing of God's will. *Then* we pray for ourselves — for forgiveness and for deliverance from evil. But, said Luther, it is quite possible to *say* the Lord's Prayer "forward" but actually *pray* it "backward." We do this when we are concerned primarily with escape from evil, misfortune, suffering, and discomfort. We start with *ourselves* — "deliver us from evil" — and think of God primarily in terms of what we want him to do for us.

A modern student of Luther and Calvin, Joseph Haroutunian, has suggested that if we want to be sure to pray the Lord's Prayer "forward" we ought to understand the familiar clauses in a radically God-centered way.

Our Father who art in heaven,	O God our Father who art not man,
Hallowed be thy name.	Make us to worship thee, and not ourselves;
Thy kingdom come,	Make us to obey thee, and not ourselves;
Thy will be done on earth as it is in heaven.	Make us to serve thee, and not ourselves.

Give us this day our daily bread.	Thou art the Giver of our daily bread — we do not earn it.
And forgive us our trespasses, as we forgive those who trespass against us.	Thou forgivest our sins, and persuadest us to love those who hate us.
And lead us not into temptation, but deliver us from evil.	Thou knowest that we are weak; Break thou the power of evil, and deliver us from sin and death.
For thine is the kingdom, and the power, and the glory forever. Amen.	For thou alone art God forever. Amen.

Now we are in a position to understand the most famous doctrine of Protestant Christianity, the doctrine of " justification by faith alone." This phrase, originally coined by the apostle Paul, summarized for the Reformers the very heart of the " good news " of the gospel which God had impelled them to rediscover. When Luther said that we are justified by *faith* and not by *works* he meant that everything comes from God. The Christian life is not a matter of winning acceptance with God — it does not depend on man's work, man's effort, man's achievement. The Christian life is a gift of God — it is a matter of the faith which God gives to man. God accepts, God loves, God takes the initiative, God awakens true faith in the minds and hearts of men. " Justification by faith alone " was a brief formulation of the revolutionary insistence of the Reformers that even within the Christian Church there is true faith and false faith, and that true faith acknowledges God's eternal priority. Justification by faith was a positive attempt to overcome the idolatry involved in self-centered religion.

One of the most convincing proofs of the fact that no aspect of Christian faith is immune to being twisted in the direction of man-centeredness is the story of what has happened to the doctrine of justification by faith in our time. Whereas Luther emphasized that faith is something God gives, we modern Protestants often look upon faith as something we achieve. How many of us really believe that religious faith is created in us by God alone and not in any sense attained by ourselves? Isn't it true that almost instinctively we shy away from any such picture of complete dependence on God? We want to be self-reliant, to demonstrate initiative, to have self-confidence. How can we develop these qualities if God demands that we take a " do nothing " attitude? We do not appreciate what we do not have to work for. If God simply hands out faith to certain individuals who throw up their hands and quit trying to establish contact with him, faith is too cheap and easy. Faith should be thought of as a result of *sincere effort*. God helps those who help themselves. On these terms what would " justification by faith " mean? We do not know, exactly, but it sounds as though it means that everything we do is influenced by our inner attitudes and that if we build up the basic attitude of faith (confidence) we shall be able to meet our problems with courage, initiative, and optimism. Everyone needs faith; faith provides power for living.

This approach to faith, which is so congenial to us, actually is a variation of the type of religion which the Protestant Reformers repudiated. It is sincere, well-intentioned, and even noble. But it opens the door to giving priority to man rather than to God. It invites us to be more concerned about ourselves and " how we are doing " than about God's glory, his greatness, and his will for us. It brings us right back to the questions that Luther and Calvin pointed at Roman Catholicism:

1. Do you seek God because faith will benefit you?

2. Do you believe that sincere moral and religious effort can build the kind of relationship to God which will bring you these benefits?

Protestant Christianity began with a two-fisted attack on forms of Christian faith that had become infected with the idolatry of self-centeredness, making God the all-powerful servant of man's desire for security and happiness. Today we Protestants must ask ourselves seriously whether our Christian faith needs reforming all over again because we have lapsed into various idolatries.

One form of idolatry among Protestants that arises out of a misdirected craving for security is worship of the Bible. Some Protestants insist that the Bible is the final authority for Christian faith and life because God inspired every word in such a way that it is absolutely free from error of any kind. In other words, the Bible is perfect, divine. Many of us appreciate the sincere concern of persons who hold this view, but we would say that the final authority for us is not the printed word but rather the living God who speaks through the Scriptures.

A form of idolatry that arises out of pride, especially group pride, is worship of some particular interpretation of the Bible and the Christian gospel. Again and again during Christian history the truth of God's revelation has had to be reinterpreted in order to be understood in the midst of changing conditions and in relation to certain definite problems. During the early days of the Protestant movement, various groups wrote " confessions " which summarized their understanding of the faith over against the Roman Catholic " errors." These Protestant confessions differed from one another in emphasis and in details, and the various groups often consigned each other to outer darkness because they claimed that only their interpretation of the Christian faith was true to the Scriptures. One of the reasons for the variety of Protestant denominations is that no single group of Christians ever has hold of the full dimensions of God's truth revealed in Christ. But, unfortunately, another reason is that churches develop vested interests in their distinctive features, and they tend to idolize themselves. Even in our own country, where differences between denominations are tolerated and church members change their affiliations quite easily, there have been and still are many Protestants who feel that their church is the only true church and that the only " real " Christians are those who conform to their understanding of the Christian message.

These might be called specialized forms of idolatry because they are tied up with special features of the Christian tradition — Bible and Church. But as we have seen in earlier chapters, the tendency to idolize important ingredients of our modern way of life, such as science and democracy and the nation, makes a powerful impact on the outlook and attitudes of Christians. The most subtle and pervasive danger of idolatry in our churches today is not centered in specialized forms like those we have mentioned, but rather in the influence of the secret gods of our age on our very conception of what the Christian faith is all about. Many of us define Christian faith in terms of the picture of ourselves and of religion that our culture offers us instead of approaching it in terms of God's distinctive revelation of himself — a revelation in which God not only defines himself but also defines us. This means that many of us are holding watered-down and adulterated conceptions of the Christian gospel which can be traced to invasions of secret gods into our faith and life. Therefore the basic issue of idolatry for us and for our churches centers around the fundamental question: What is Christianity?

CHAPTER

7

"MAKING THE MOST OF YOURSELF" CHRISTIANITY

What is Christianity? Suppose we asked the Gallup Poll to sample the opinions of all the Americans who attend Protestant church services on any one Sunday. A composite summary probably would look something like this:

Beneath all the jargon of creed and doctrine, beneath all the pomp of ceremony and ritual, the secret power of Christianity always has been the appeal of the ideals Jesus taught and the inspiration of his wonderful life. The genius of Christianity lies in the fact that although God is hidden behind the dim unknown, Jesus is out in the open where we can see him. We can become acquainted with Jesus by reading the Gospels, and in becoming acquainted with him we become acquainted with God. Jesus revealed God's will in his teaching, and he demonstrated God's concern for the infinite value of human personality in his way of dealing with people. Therefore we worship God in spirit and in truth when we give our full devotion to Jesus and sincerely accept his way of life as our own. A true Christian is a person who practices what Jesus preached.

To put it in a single sentence, American Protestants tend to define Christian faith as a "way of life" based on the moral ideals Jesus taught and the good life Jesus lived.

Certainly Jesus Christ is the center of Christian faith, and certainly Jesus as teacher and example is indispensable to Christians. Yet this is not all that the Bible and Christian tradition tell us about Jesus, and it is not even the most important part of the Christian gospel. Primary concentration on Jesus' way of life has encouraged modern Protestants to fall into a state of abysmal ignorance concerning the total, over-all message of the Bible and Christian tradition. It has led to a dangerously one-sided interpretation of Jesus Christ, of the God whom Christ revealed, and of the character of human living in relation to God. It has provided an effective loophole for idolatry.

Recently the tie-up between a one-sided understanding of Jesus Christ and idolatry was discussed rather heatedly in the very first meeting of a midweek Bible study group. Those present were Mrs. Wilson, Mr. Brown, Mr. Knox, Miss Peters, and Rev. Mr. Parke. The discussion broke out immediately after Mr. Parke had challenged the group by saying:

" Many churches accept into their membership any person who will state publicly that he accepts Jesus Christ as his Lord and Savior. What is involved in this affirmation? I am going to ask four questions which I hope will stimulate us in our discussion of what Christian faith is all about. Listen to them very closely.

" 1. Is Jesus called ' Lord ' simply because he is a teacher who shows us how to live?

" 2. Is Jesus called ' Savior ' simply because he is an example who inspires us to live as we ought to live?

" 3. When Jesus said, ' I and the Father are one,' was he merely saying that because he lived up to certain moral ideals he had achieved fellowship with God?

" 4. When Jesus said, ' No one comes to the Father, but by

me,' was he merely saying that unless we make a serious effort to apply his teachings to our daily living we shall not achieve fellowship with God the way he did? "

MRS. WILSON: Mr. Parke, you have slanted your questions in a way that is very irritating to me. As soon as you begin hinting that Jesus was more than a human person like ourselves, you are going down the road toward worshiping Jesus instead of God. If calling Jesus Lord and Savior means that we have to worship him and pray to him, I will have to bow out because I cannot honestly pray to Jesus.

REV. MR. PARKE: Thank you for being so frank, Mrs. Wilson. I believe that you are aware of a genuine danger of idolatry. Many Christians tend to indulge in a Jesus cult, worshiping the historical personality of Jesus. The writer of the Gospel of John reports that Jesus once cautioned his followers against this very tendency. He tells us that Jesus cried out emphatically, " He who believes in me, believes not in me but in him who sent me " (John 12:44). This is a striking statement. It is as though Jesus was saying: " Do not make my personality the center of your faith. If you focus your devotion on Jesus of Nazareth, you will be worshiping a human being and not God."

MR. BROWN (*breaking in*): Now *I* am the one who is irritated. If I remember my religious training correctly, I was taught that in Jesus, God was expressing himself in a human life. Jesus did not merely tell us that " God is love." He was that divine love in action.

MRS. WILSON: But, Mr. Brown, even if Jesus was a perfect example of what love looks like in human living, he still was a man and not God. God isn't human personality raised to the nth degree. I want to love God and the people around me the way Jesus did, but God comes first, not Jesus.

REV. MR. PARKE: A few moments ago I seemed to side with

Mrs. Wilson, but now I am going to support Mr. Brown's position by quoting once again from the Gospel of John. The Gospel writer summarizes his faith in the opening paragraphs of his book, where he talks about the " Word " of God as the creative power by which God created the heavens and the earth. Now listen to what he says: " The Word became flesh and dwelt among us." God's creative power became a human being like us. John closes his summary with this sentence: " No one has ever seen God; the only Son, who is in the bosom of the Father, he has made him known."

I think this indicates that strangely enough the writer of the Fourth Gospel agrees with Mrs. Wilson that Jesus of Nazareth is not to be made a substitute for God, and yet he also agrees with Mr. Brown that Jesus is more than just a carpenter and teacher and leader of men. There is a mystery about Jesus.

MR. KNOX: This discussion is well on its way toward becoming boringly theological. You have turned Jesus into a puzzle, and soon all the old traditional doctrines will come prancing out again. I am a practical man and I believe that Christianity offers a simple, practical approach to life. The real issue is this: What are we human beings here on this earth for anyway? I believe that the purpose of my life is to become the kind of person God made me to be, that is, to reach my potential. Now, what is my potential? God has put Jesus out in front of me as the ideal toward which he wants me to move. If I apply the principles of Jesus to my affairs, I will progress toward true goodness and true happiness. If I loaf on the job or deny these principles, I will be cutting myself off from realizing my potential and my life will not be truly satisfying. This is the real challenge and I try to meet it. Why do you theologians always complicate Christianity?

REV. MR. PARKE: Theology shouldn't bore you, Mr. Knox. You have just made a thoroughly theological statement. Whenever we think about the meaning and purpose of our lives we are in the realm of theology whether we know it or not. The question for us Christians always is whether our theology is *fully* Christian — by which I mean, faithful to the over-all message of the Scriptures — or whether it is a narrowed-down, one-sided version of the gospel.

I do not want to make Christianity complicated. I believe that the message of the Bible is quite simple, basically. But it is not simple in the way you think it is.

MR. KNOX: You will have to show me.

REV. MR. PARKE: Well, I don't think I can *show* you, but I can point out some serious difficulties in your idea that Christianity boils down to following Jesus. For instance, if you are facing a decision and the alternatives are not clear-cut black and white, how do you answer the question, " What would Jesus do? "

MR. KNOX: That's what the Gospels are for. They tell us what Jesus was like.

REV. MR. PARKE: I don't think you realize how little we actually know about Jesus. Ever since modern methods of studying past history were developed, a search for the *real* Jesus has been going on. Never before have so many people devoted so many years to the quest for an accurate picture of one person as Christian scholars have given to the effort to penetrate into the personality of Jesus. Yet out of all this work has come the realization that the Gospels give us a picture perforated by big gaps. We have no way of arriving at a " practical " conception of Jesus' personality except to fill in the gaps with our own imagination, or to accept someone else's imaginative picture.

MRS. WILSON: Why, that's fantastic! I have always taken for granted that if there is any person who lived long ago whom we know intimately, it is Jesus.

MR. KNOX: I certainly agree with you, Mrs. Wilson, and I

think that most of the members of our church feel the same way.

REV. MR. PARKE: I'm not sure they do. It seems to me that a great many of us need to reconsider our relationship to Jesus as a man who lived in Palestine two thousand years ago. Let me back up what I just said by telling you about a study Albert Schweitzer made before he decided to become a missionary doctor and to establish a hospital in Africa. Schweitzer read dozens of "Lives of Jesus" written during the nineteenth century, and by comparing them he discovered that each generation of scholars found its own thoughts in Jesus. He found that each man who wrote a life of Jesus created a picture that revealed his own character. I can repeat one sentence he wrote word for word, because it gave me such a shock when I read it for the first time. Here is what he said: "There is no historical task which so reveals a man's true self as the writing of a Life of Jesus."

MRS. WILSON: Do you mean to say that everyone who reads the story of Jesus simply finds what he wants to find?

REV. MR. PARKE: I wouldn't go so far as to say that. But the danger is always there, and this is especially true when we center our attention mainly on the human personality of Jesus, as though this were the heart of the Christian message. It seems to me that if we concentrate on trying to picture the personality of Jesus in order to answer the question, "What would Jesus do?" we are likely to end up with a Jesus idol made in our own image — a picture that reflects the ideas about human personality which we have picked up unconsciously from the life of our own time and not from the Bible.

MR. KNOX: This idol business is a lot of nonsense as far as I am concerned. I don't set up Jesus as an idol patterned after myself. Now that I come to think of it, when I ask myself what Jesus would do in a certain situation, I think mainly about his teachings, his blueprint for life. You can argue all you like about " the facts " — whether Jesus did this first or that first or whether he did it at all, and so on — but still the Sermon on the Mount remains a solid rock. It's a fact. You can take it or leave it, but you cannot say that you merely imagined it.

Miss Peters: I hesitate to speak because what I want to say will make it seem as though our group is splitting into two factions. But I do not agree with the idea that the Christian faith centers around realizing our potential as defined by the Sermon on the Mount. I believe it centers around that fact that we continually fail to come even close to living up to it. When I compare my actual living with Jesus' teachings, I am driven to the wall, so to speak.

Mrs. Wilson: My dear, you are much too hard on yourself. You create unnecessary feelings of frustration because you do not understand what an ideal is. An ideal is not something we actually achieve, at least if it is an ideal of becoming perfect. The purpose of an ideal such as Jesus taught is to keep us growing, stretching, moving toward the best that is in us. That is what God wants us to do.

Miss Peters: I beg to differ with you, Mrs. Wilson. You are opening a back door which allows us to escape the seriousness of God's demands on us. Jesus did not say anything about doing our best and letting it go at that. He said we *must* be perfect. And he even went beyond saying we should be like him. He said we must be perfect as our Father in heaven is perfect. We have no right to suppose that God will accept us simply because we are well-meaning individuals who try to be good. How do we know when we are truly sincere? It is easy to fool ourselves about this. And how do we measure whether we actually are doing our very best? Our imagination can play clever tricks, especially when we would like to think well of ourselves.

Mrs. Wilson: As my husband would say, you insist on putting yourself behind the eight ball. You simply won't allow yourself to be optimistic and confident. I think it is very unhealthy to be suspicious of your sincerity and your motives.

MISS PETERS: And I think it is unhealthy to be optimistic and self-confident when such attitudes cover up what is really going on in our living.

REV. MR. PARKE: Perhaps we ought to ask Miss Peters to tell us what the Christian faith means to her. Could you tell us in a few words?

MISS PETERS: I'll try. I believe that unless we love God with *all* our heart, soul, strength, and mind — our neighbor as ourselves — we shall perish in the hell of our own self-centeredness. I also believe that every one of us is in this kind of hell. And besides that, I believe that unless God comes into hell to get us out we won't get out. We are terribly confused if we think that calling Jesus our teacher and example is the same as calling him our Lord and Savior. Jesus is our Lord and Savior because in Jesus, God himself was taking the necessary steps to free us from the hell of lovelessness we create by being so everlastingly self-centered.

MR. KNOX: Aren't you being melodramatic? Undoubtedly you are speaking on the basis of some deeply moving experiences, but I certainly do not feel that I am in hell. I feel that I am an unfinished product, on the road toward becoming completed, perfected. So far as self-centeredness is concerned, I agree that it is a problem — one might even say it is a hell of a problem, as you suggest — but as we become responsible adults we learn to curb our selfishness and to serve others. My motto is, "God first, others second, myself third." If a person keeps this motto in his mind constantly, it is bound to help him be less selfish.

MR. BROWN: I haven't said anything for a long time because I have been interested in the clash of points of view, and at the same time I have been thinking about this business of idolatry. The crucial question, it seems to me, is this: What is the purpose of human living? Which comes first, the purpose of praising God and living in fellowship with him, or the purpose of becoming our "best self" as far as possible? If the purpose of life is to realize our potential, as Mr. Knox has said, then the center of concern very easily — I would even say, inevitably — turns out to be *ourselves*. No matter how heatedly we may argue that God is central because it is he who has set up the true pattern of living, or because it is God who sent Jesus to make this pattern known to us, the real focus of interest lies in our sincere efforts to become the kind of persons we believe we ought to be. Even while we pray to God to help us grow toward our ideals, it is ourselves we are most concerned about.

Mr. Knox: In other words, you are saying that when I make my motto, "God first, others second, myself third" this is just so much window dressing!

Mr. Brown: Well, yes, in a way. I do not see how any religion that puts primary emphasis on "being good" or "making the most of ourselves" can avoid getting locked up in self-centeredness.

But actually, the same criticism hits me too, because in one way or another all of us are idolaters who worship at the shrine of self. In fact, it occurs to me that if we want to see what an idol looks like, all we have to do is to look in a mirror!

Rev. Mr. Parke (*after a pause*): As you see, Mr. Brown, you have reduced us to silence and self-examination. You have pushed beneath the surface of our discussion to the most fundamental of all religious issues: Whom do we *actually* worship?

I am sure that all of us want to honor God's priority. The question Mr. Brown has raised is whether our understanding of the Christian faith allows God to be *God* — whether our theology guards against subordinating God to our quest for happiness and personal fulfillment. No understanding of the gospel is foolproof — or I should say, idol-proof. To put it in an extreme way, it is entirely possible for me to idolize myself proudly because I think I have such keen insight into the problem of idolatry — and probably I do. Yet it is better to hold a view which constantly reminds us of the danger of idolatry than it is to hold a view that does not take it seriously. And not only is it better in the sense of being wiser, but also it is more faithful to the Biblical story of God's dealing with mankind and more faithful to the over-all understanding of life which has been the mainstream of Christian tradition.

MR. KNOX: Here we go again. Is there such a thing as one "over-all understanding of life" in the Bible and Christian tradition? You keep talking about being faithful to the Bible and Christian tradition. This leaves me unconvinced because there have been many traditions, and my own approach to Christianity is one of them. Which tradition?

REV. MR. PARKE: I am glad that you have brought up this question in such a clear-cut way. It is very much to the point. In order to answer it, however, I shall have to break up our discussion for a while and launch into a sort of lecture. Are you people willing to make such a shift? You are? Fine. This will take some time, but I believe that it will be worth it. The theme I am going to develop might be called "the tradition within the traditions."

8

THE TRADITION WITHIN THE TRADITIONS

During the last several generations we Protestants have tended to cut and trim Christianity to fit the optimistic, progressive temper of our modern cultural tradition. One fundamental feature of this tradition is the belief that there is nothing wrong with us human beings that additional knowledge, wider education, and better scientific techniques cannot cope with. And beneath this belief is the conviction that we are the kind of beings who can do what we ought to do if we seriously devote ourselves to doing what we ought to do. You see, what I am saying is that our faith in human goodness belongs more to modern culture than to Christianity. This faith has infiltrated our religious life so effectively that we take it for granted as though it were a part of " Christian tradition."

The Bible does not agree with us. It presents a picture of life — essentially the same from Genesis to Revelation — which must be understood if the Christian gospel is to be understood. Let us look at the book of Genesis, for instance. From a strictly historical point of view, it brings together a variety of materials that give a background for the birth of the Hebrew nation. But Genesis is not a strictly historical book. It is theological. It explains *why* the Hebrew nation was brought into being, and the explanation is religious. The man (or men) who arranged

the sequence of materials built them into a dramatic structure
which sets the stage for the entire unfolding of Biblical history, including Jesus Christ and the founding of the Christian
Church.

What is the structure of Genesis? "In the beginning God
created the heavens and the earth." The description of creation
reaches its climax in the appearance on the scene of man and
woman (in Hebrew "Adam" means "man"; "Eve" means
"woman"). "And God saw everything that he had made,
and behold, it was very good." *But* immediately the goodness
is spoiled by the very creatures whom God has endowed most
richly with abilities and responsibilities. Trouble arises at the
peak of creation because Adam and Eve deny their fellowship
with God in favor of having their own way. They are not
satisfied to be God's creatures. They aspire to overcome their
limitations and to become the sole judges of good and evil.
They introduce idolatry into God's world by preferring themselves to God.

A continuing crisis is produced in the relationship between
God and man which causes innumerable crises in the life of
men with one another. Not only are Adam and Eve driven
from the Garden of Eden, but as human society develops men
grow so wicked that God is pictured as being sorry he ever
created human beings. He resolves that a new beginning must
be attempted. By means of a great flood civilization is wiped
out and only Noah and his family remain to found society
all over again.

But the same thing happens. This time the climax of idolatry
is reached in the project of building a tower that will reach
from earth to heaven, the so-called Tower of Babel. This proud
and ambitious project is a marvelous symbol of our lust to be
self-sufficient, our yearning to be the master of our fate by
bringing all aspects of life under our control. The penalty this

time is misunderstanding, estrangement, confusion, loss of fellowship and community. Mankind is split up into groups which live in enmity and constant strife.

What is God going to do? The book of Genesis suddenly shifts its attention to a certain man named Abraham and to certain of his descendants. God calls Abraham as a special agent of his purpose. Abraham has two sons, Ishmael and Isaac. God calls Isaac. Isaac has two sons, Esau and Jacob. God calls Jacob. Jacob has twelve sons. God forms the Hebrew people out of the descendants of these men. God's " new beginning " in human history is the creation of a special people which is to make God known to all men, to call them into true fellowship with him, and in this way to lay the foundation for true community with one another.

This is the " theological drama " that is expressed in the structure of Genesis. In one sense this drama happened " once upon a time," but in a deeper sense it is a description of human existence in all times and places. The basic crisis in the relationship between God and man is the background against which the rest of the Bible " makes sense." And the Bible as a whole can " make sense " to us only if we realize that you and I are Adam and Eve. We are causing the same crisis in our generation which the people in the book of Genesis caused in their several generations. And the peculiar character of the difficulty is the same also. We say to ourselves: " I will play the part of God in my life. I will be the center of my world." We put something less than God in the place of God and separate ourselves from fellowship with the source and meaning of our life.

We do not idolize ourselves because we are ignorant. We know very well that we did not create the world and that we are not " self-made " men and women. We know that we are dependent on processes and persons far beyond the range of our control. We know that we are creatures, doomed to die after a brief span of years, and that after we are gone the world will get along quite well without us.

We do not idolize ourselves because we are descended from the animal kingdom and have not yet overcome our brutish origins. Self-centeredness requires a quality of freedom and a capacity for imagining and reasoning which not even the highest animals enjoy. Idolatry is a peculiarly human achievement.

We do not idolize ourselves because we have strong physical impulses which conquer our spiritual impulses. The desire to want our own way, to try to bend the universe around our fingers, to make ourselves the center of life, is rooted in our "spirit" and not in our body. Its home is the core of our personality where attitudes and motives originate. Idolatry stems from the misuse of our highest and noblest capacities.

According to the Bible, we say, "I will play the part of God in my life," because we really do not trust God. We are anxious about ourselves. If we trusted God completely, we would give ourselves confidently to him and to our neighbor in love. But as a matter of fact, we are afraid of "losing our life" and this fear goads us into making desperate efforts to "save our life" by drawing the universe around ourselves.

This idolatrous situation is what the Bible calls *sin*. Sin is not *sins,* certain acts that are "bad." Sin is a condition of life which affects all levels of living. It is a fundamental dislocation of the whole of life. Jesus described sin when he said, "Out of the heart of man come evil thoughts, fornication, theft, murder, adultery, coveting, wickedness, deceit, licentiousness, envy, slander, pride, foolishness" (Mark 7:21, 22). By the *heart* Jesus meant the core of personality, the center of the self where attitudes and motives influence our decisions. Paul made the same point in one of his lists of the "works of the flesh." He emphasized "spiritual" actions like idolatry, strife, enmity, jealousy, anger, selfishness, dissension, party spirit, envy, and the like more than "physical" actions such as immorality, drunkenness, licentiousness, and carousing (Gal. 5:19–21). This means that getting drunk, for example, is not so much wrong in itself as it is an indication that something is wrong in the total life of the person who drinks excessively. It is a symptom of sin. The cause lies in the heart — in the center of a personality that is desperate and restless because of its separation from God.

Some of us express our self-centeredness through one or another form of sensuality. Most of us Protestants probably do not. But since idolatry affects the very core of our being, we simply express it in other ways — perhaps in our religion! Why do you suppose that Jesus reserved his most scathing criticisms for the best church members of his day, the Pharisees? He told them bluntly, "You are like whitewashed tombs, which outwardly appear beautiful, but within they are full of dead men's bones and all uncleanness" (Matt. 23:27). Jesus saw that religion is the most dangerous of all human activities because it is the highest, most noble, and all-inclusive expression of human living. Precisely because we seek meaning and purpose for the whole of life through religion, religion presents the greatest opportunity for selfishness. Religion can be our grandest attempt to win that security for ourselves which we crave and which we realize cannot be achieved on any less comprehensive level of life.

The Bible from beginning to end describes human living as a wonderful and good thing which is spoiled. All men are sinners, which does not mean that every one of us is mean and dirty and low, but rather that every one of us tries to play God. *And the decisive fact is that nothing we can do will change the situation, for everything that we do is affected by the heart which needs to be changed.* We are bound to dislike what the Bible tells us about ourselves, but unless we accept the " bad news " of sin we never shall understand the " good news " which is the mystery and glory of the Christian faith. The message of the entire Bible centers around God's " strategy " for dealing with our idolatry, and it reaches its climax in Jesus Christ.

Now at this point I want to emphasize once again that our tendency to narrow our attention to the life and teachings of Jesus makes it difficult if not impossible to see what the Christian faith is all about. The fact is that the life and teachings of Jesus were only one part of the " good news " which the early Christians preached and which those who heard them accepted.

What was the message that the earliest Christians preached to persons who were not yet members of the Church? One of the most important discoveries that has been made recently in the field of New Testament research is the difference between *teaching* and *preaching* in the life of the Early Church. We have come to recognize that the New Testament was written for people who already were Christians. It was a handbook of the faith and was used for teaching. But scholars have found fragments of the earliest *preaching* hidden in Paul's letters and in speeches of the apostle Peter reported in the book of The Acts. When Christians told non-Christians about their faith they emphasized three themes:

1. Jesus was the Christ, the holy one of God promised in Hebrew prophecy and prepared for in the religious history of mankind.

2. The life, death, resurrection, and exaltation of Jesus were all one great act of God for the sake of delivering men from sin.

3. All men are summoned to turn from their self-centered

ways, to accept the forgiveness and reconciliation with God made possible in Christ, and to give themselves to a new life whose chief characteristic will be the presence of Christ within them (as God's Holy Spirit) as a power for righteousness.

If we study the structure of the Gospels, we shall find that they are expanded versions of these three themes. If we study the various letters written by Paul and others, we shall find that they use various words and expressions to communicate and explain the very same three major themes. The New Testament does not concentrate on Jesus as teacher and example first of all, but rather on the one great act of God in and through Jesus by which God himself broke through the barrier of idolatry we men erect around ourselves and opened up the possibility of reunion. Once men have been restored to fellowship with God, *then* the teaching and example of Jesus play an important role in guiding the new life that has been created. But this places " Jesus' way of life " in a very different framework from the one we use when we think that Jesus represents our ideal and that Christianity is just a matter of sincerely applying his principles to our affairs.

The message about Jesus Christ which was the essence of Christianity for the earliest Christians focused not on what Jesus said and did but on *who* he was. And in trying to explain who Jesus was, they made the very kind of estimate of Jesus that someone has charged " turns Jesus into a puzzle." They found it necessary to insist that Jesus was both God and man, both human and divine.

On the one hand, they all affirmed that " Jesus is Lord " (God) and transferred to him words used in the Old Testament of God alone. They prayed to Jesus and to God in the name of Jesus, while still believing that there is only one God.

On the other hand, they all affirmed that Jesus was a man, a historical personality. They did not hold that Jesus knew

everything and could do anything he pleased. They insisted
that Jesus really got tired, hungry, discouraged, and lonely like
any other normal person.

We can take it for granted, I think, that the early Christians
knew perfectly well that they were making astounding claims
about Jesus. Yet they dared to assert that in the life, death, and
resurrection of this man God himself was present in a unique
way, so that if we want to see clearly who God is and what he
has done, we are to look at this man Jesus. But, you see, we
are not to look at him as "the best man who ever lived" or
as "the most profound teacher of morals in human history."
We are to look at him as *God in action,* as God uttering an
eternal "No!" against our persistent idolatry and yet, at the
very same time, uttering a victorious "Yes!" in favor of wel-
coming us into fellowship with himself in spite of our idolatry
and of renewing a right spirit within us.

I have been presenting what I feel is the mainstream of
Christian faith, and now I should like to summarize what we
have been talking about and to draw some conclusions.

1. We have discussed the contention that a narrowed-down
or one-sided understanding of the Christian faith leads us in
the direction of idolatry without our realizing the danger. We
have questioned the adequacy of much present-day Protestant
religion because (*a*) it does not appreciate the message of the
whole Bible, especially the Old Testament, about the crisis in
the relation between God and men which has faced every generation from the beginning until now; and because (*b*) it does
not take into account the witness of the *whole* New Testament
regarding who Jesus was and what God did in and through
him to meet the crisis.

2. We have suggested that the inadequacy of much of our
Protestant religion can be pin-pointed by looking carefully at
what we believe about ourselves. Do we think of ourselves as

capable of living according to the ideal of "God first, others second, myself last"? Our dynamic, progressive, successful modern culture conditions us to say yes. Yet in the light of the Bible and Christian tradition, this very notion that we can achieve love of God and our neighbor if we really try hard enough is an evidence of idolatry. It disregards the fact that every one of us misuses his great gifts and capacities in the interest of getting his own way and of trying to gain security by playing God in his own little world.

3. There is one question we have not yet asked. What is the conception of God which results from this side-stepping of the facts of life? The result is that we construct a picture that fits in with our ideas and desires and prejudices — a narrowed-down, one-sided conception of God.

We think of God as an interested spectator who applauds our efforts to become fine, generous, well-adjusted persons and who is terribly disappointed when we become careless or in-different. We do not like the old, tough-minded idea of God as an impartial divine lawgiver. The penalty for failure used to be hell-fire and brimstone, but nowadays we breathe quite easily because we tell ourselves that since God is gentle and mild like Jesus — and whose imaginary picture of Jesus really is this? — he never would inflict such punishment on anyone. But our modern God is more than a spectator. We picture him as our Friend who always is ready, able, and willing to step in and lend us a hand whenever we think we need help. Or we consider God our Senior Partner; he needs our collabora-tion in the building of a better world, and we need his aid in the building of well-adjusted personalities. God counts on us, and we count on him.

What has become of the majestic power of the God who created the heavens and the earth, in whose sight the nations are as a drop in a bucket? What has become of the uncanny mystery of the God whose thoughts are not our thoughts and whose ways are not our ways? Where is the severity of the divine Judge who demands our complete and unswerving loyalty, who knows us better than we know ourselves and who is not deceived by our clever maneuverings to combine what we want with " doing God's will "? You see, we want to know the God who is our Friend without meeting him as the enemy of our idolatry. We want to experience the fact that " the eternal God is our refuge, and underneath are the everlasting arms " without experiencing the fact that " it is a terrible thing [a shattering experience] to fall into the hands of the living God."

I am absolutely certain that much of our Protestant religion is built on a blasphemous conception of God as an indulgent Father who merely asks us to give a little time and effort to " the Christian way of life " and who winks at our halfhearted loyalty. This God is an idol. He is a product of our wishful thinking, a tool of our self-seeking, a reflection of our self-indulgence. The question that haunts me again and again is whether many of us are ever really confronted by the living God in the midst of our well-meaning, conventional efforts to be Christians. I am convinced that God is at work among us continually, but how many of us recognize God's " strange work " of unmasking our self-worship and our inadequate conceptions of his greatness? If we don't, we can be sure that the full impact of God's revelation of himself has not yet grasped and reshaped the core of our being. We can be sure that we are defining Christianity in terms of ourselves and our man-centered culture rather than coming to terms with God's definition of himself and of us.

Then what does it mean to be a Christian? A Christian is a person who is confronted by the living God in such a way that he becomes aware both of God's demand for undivided loyalty and of his own divided loyalties. A Christian is a person who acknowledges that he does not give God *effective priority* in his living.

Is this all it means to be a Christian? Where are the joy, peace, and fullness of life which fellowship with God is supposed to create? They are *on the other side* of an encounter with God in which it becomes clear that God does not conform to what we normally hope and expect and deeply desire. The glory of the Christian message is that God is a God who *comes* — he has come into our life in spite of our preoccupation with our pet interests and concerns, and he will come again. But the disturbing seriousness of the Christian message is that true faith involves suffering as the price of new life; it involves being willing to live in the midst of a permanent revolution. Again and again God's creative activity must subject the Christian to painful recognition of his divided and idolatrous loyalties in order that he may experience the mystery and the wonder of God's everlasting love.

Certainly there is more to the Christian life than mere acknowledgment of idolatry. The point we have been trying to make is that Christian joy and peace and fullness of life grow out of the realization that *by the grace of God revealed in Jesus Christ* the Christian is a *forgiven idolater,* an idolater who is accepted *as he is* into fellowship. The power and the courage and the confidence for continued battling with his own self-centeredness and with the group idolatries of his society are rooted in glad thankfulness for the fact that nothing — not even his idolatry — can separate him from the love of God, from God's grace, offered freely in Jesus Christ.

CHAPTER 9

Where Do We Go from Here?

We modern Protestant Christians have not evolved to a higher stage where false loyalties no longer tempt us. We cannot understand what is going on in our own hearts and minds, or in the lives of other people, unless we see that the struggle for loyalty is just as real today as it was when the Hebrew prophets attacked the fertility gods of soil and sex in the name of God the Creator, when the early Christians attacked the Greek and Roman gods in the name of Jesus Christ, and when the Reformers attacked distortions of Christian faith within the Church itself in the name of the God who says, " You shall have no other gods before me."

It is true that the Biblical drama came to its climax in Jesus Christ, and that the Christian Church grew out of the fuller revelation which Christ brought. But this did not settle the issue of idolatry. *It made idolatry more evident than ever.* For since God made himself known more fully in Christ than anywhere else, Christians have less excuse than anyone else for failing to spot idolatrous loyalties. Christ opened a new way to reconciliation with God, but he did not relieve his followers of temptations to worship themselves or the works of their hands or the movements and programs which are important in their society. That is a battle they have to fight, and it never is settled once for all.

What resources are needed? One thing is clear: false loyalties can be recognized only in the light of true loyalty. There must be a " yardstick." This yardstick consists of the fundamental convictions concerning God and man which are central to the Bible and Christian tradition. These convictions must be relearned year by year and generation by generation. They cannot be taken for granted. And so far as Protestants are concerned, the task of getting hold of the yardstick in its full dimensions is not the duty of ministers and scholars alone, but the duty of *every* Christian.

Now, how can we understand the gospel unless we " think about God " deeply and seriously and carefully? But to " think about God " means *theology,* and our troubles begin right away, because most of us have a strong aversion to theology. We consider it abstract and theoretical, something that gets in the way of making religion effective in practical living. We are impatient with careful analyses and clear-cut distinctions in the realm of faith. We suspect that too much thinking about faith kills it. We also suspect that concern with theology leads to narrow dogmatism and intolerance.

There is some basis for some of these reservations. As we have seen, there is literally no aspect of the Christian life that is immune to distortion and misuse. Nevertheless, we cannot develop the ability to recognize the idols that challenge Christian faith in American culture, inside the churches — and inside us! — if we are unwilling to do serious theological work. We must take the risks involved in disciplined thinking and in holding views that have sharp edges. Theology is no substitute for faith, but faith cannot get along without it if it is to be faithful. Christian theology is simply the never-ending effort to keep hold of *all* of the essentials of God's revelation of himself. Actually, flabby tolerance and vague thinking about God and the life of faith are theological too, but here the struggle for truth has been given up and the understanding of the gospel is certain to be watered-down, one-sided, and open to the confusion that leads to idolatry.

If being a Christian involves never-ending concern about letting God be *God* and giving him our deepest loyalty, then we are highly *impractical* unless we search continually for a vital, full-fledged, consistent theological understanding of what the Bible and Christian tradition tell us about God and about what is involved in being loyal to him.

A hundred years ago a concerned Christian layman named Sören Kierkegaard wrote a parable about the conventional faith characteristic of his fellow church members in Denmark. It is just as fresh and challenging today as it was then, and it is just as applicable to American Protestants as it was to Danish Protestants. Here is the parable:

The Tame Geese

" Suppose it was so that the geese could talk — then they had so arranged it that they also could have their religious worship, their divine service.

" Every Sunday they came together, and one of the ganders preached. The essential content of the sermon was: what a lofty destiny the geese had, what a high goal the Creator (and every time this word was mentioned the geese curtsied and the ganders bowed the head) had set before the geese; by the aid of wings they could fly away to distant regions, blessed climes, where properly they were at home, for here they were only strangers.

" So it was every Sunday. And as soon as the assembly broke up each waddled home to his own affairs. And then the next Sunday again to divine worship and then again home — and that was the end of it; they throve and were well-liking, became plump and delicate — and then were eaten on Martinmas

Eve — and that was the end of it.

"That was the end of it. For though the discourse sounded so lofty on Sunday, the geese on Monday were ready to recount to one another what befell a goose that had wanted to make serious use of the wings the Creator had given him, designed for the high goal that was proposed to him — what befell him, what a terrible death he encountered.

"[Also] among the geese there were some individuals which seemed suffering and grew thin. About them it was currently said among the geese: There you see what it leads to when flying is taken seriously. For because their hearts are occupied with the thought of wanting to fly, therefore they become thin, do not thrive, do not have the grace of God as we have who therefore become plump and delicate.

"And then when someone reads this he says: It is very pretty — and that's the end of it. Then he waddles home to his affairs, becomes (or at least endeavors with all his might to become) plump, delicate, fat — but on Sunday morning the parson preachifies . . . and he listens . . . always like the geese."

References

In this volume reference is made to the following books and periodicals, which are listed in the order of their use:

Chapter 1

Lloyd and Mary Morain, *Humanism as the Next Step*. The Beacon Press, 1954.

D. Elton Trueblood, "The New Comparative Religion," *The Interseminary Series,* Vol. II. Harper & Brothers, 1946.

Chapter 3

Will Herberg, *Protestant — Catholic — Jew*. Doubleday & Co., Inc., 1955.

Time magazine, August 18, 1947, pp. 74, 77.

Joseph Ratner, ed., *Intelligence in the Modern World: John Dewey's Philosophy*. Random House, Inc., 1939.

Will Herberg, "The Biblical Basis of American Democracy," *Thought,* Vol. XXX, No. 116, Spring, 1955.

Joshua Loth Liebman, *Peace of Mind*. Simon & Schuster, Inc., 1946.

Chapter 5

Norman Vincent Peale, *The Power of Positive Thinking*. Prentice-Hall, Inc., 1952.

Billy Graham, *Peace with God*. Doubleday & Co., Inc., 1955.

Donald Meyer, "Billy Graham — and Success," *The New Republic,* August 22, 1955.

Chapter 6

Philip S. Watson, *Let God Be God!* Muhlenberg Press, 1948.

Joseph Haroutunian, *Wisdom and Folly in Religion*. Charles Scribner's Sons, 1940.

Chapter 9

Walter Lowrie, *Kierkegaard*. Oxford University Press, 1938.